YOU'RE AS HEALED AS YOU ARE SAVED

How To Get Miracle-Working Faith
When All The Formulas Fail

by Pastor John Stocker

Unless otherwise indicated all Scripture quotations are taken from the New King James Version of the Bible.

ISBN 1-931527-25-3

Printed in the United States

Edited by Larry Witten

Cover design by Liz Malwitz Design

TABLE OF CONTENTS

FOREWORD

================

This isn't just *another* book about faith or a "how-to" manual on healing. This book is the story of my personal search for a faith that could save my life...and it contains what God taught me.

For many years, I had pastored a large non-denominational church made up primarily of charismatic people who believed the faith message, as I did. Then came a period of several years, during which I was diagnosed with three diseases, each of which could potentially take my life. That was when I discovered that, although I had embraced the faith teaching, I still lacked faith for my healing.

When I became truly desperate and cried out to God, He showed me how to believe for my miracle. What I learned was not only how to have faith for healing, but how to have faith for *every* need. This truth has literally preserved my life.

Let me go back to the beginning and tell you how this all started. During the last half of the twentieth century, God restored to His people many truths concerning faith. He caused powerful ministries to rise up with a fresh understanding of faith's role in our lives.

The first "faith book" I read was entitled, *How Faith Works* by Dr. Fred Price. It was a simple book, yet it had a profound effect upon my life. Although I had been in full-time ministry for more than fifteen years, I discovered that I didn't understand the role God wanted faith to play in my life. Along with many other believers, I began an exciting *walk of faith* that produced many miracles and brought glory to God.

After a number of years, I began to notice a disturbing pattern among faith people. It seemed that when it came to actually receiving miracles, more people *failed* than succeeded. In fact, most of the funerals I conducted were for people who died "standing in faith" to be healed.

As time went on, I noticed more and more people were rejecting the "faith message" because they or a loved one had failed to receive a miracle.

Faith teachers were quick to point out that two things can cause you not to receive: never having faith in the first place or allowing Satan to steal it. I totally agree. God's Word is clear, *real faith always produces a miracle.* Nowhere in the Bible can I find a single exception. *Real* faith *always* works!

So, I began to ask myself, "Why is it that some people don't have *real* faith?" Then I became aware of a curious fact—the people who *failed* to receive a miracle seemed to have done all the right things. They continually read and quoted scripture to feed their faith. They "claimed" and consistently "confessed" their miracle.

In fact, much to my surprise, those who did not receive from God actually appeared to be more diligent than those who did. It became apparent that something must be missing from our understanding of faith. I wondered, "What was the missing ingredient?"

I was still bewildered when it came time to seek God for my own healing. In the months that followed, I went through some very dark and difficult times. Struggling with three deadly diseases, I knew I was dying. The only question seemed to be which disease would get me first.

Then God taught me how to have *real* faith. I must confess that I wasn't a very quick learner, but God stuck with me until "I got it." During this process, I learned two vitally important things: first—ANY CHRISTIAN CAN LIVE BY FAITH; second—THERE IS A KIND OF FAITH THAT *ALWAYS WORKS*—100 times out of 100—in every circumstance and situation of life!

God isn't the problem when we fail to receive our miracle—He is ready, willing, and able to answer our prayers. In fact, three times in the Bible God tells us "the just shall live by faith." The problem is with our understanding of how to have true or *real* faith.

If you want to live by faith but don't know how…if you feel like faith should work every time but it doesn't for you…or if you've given up on faith entirely—you've tried it and been disappointed—then I wrote this book for you. When you turn this page, you will begin a quest to discover *real* faith for your every need.

CHAPTER 1

FAITH WITHOUT FAIL

Faith saved me from an early death. I had been diagnosed with three life-threatening incurable diseases and had been seriously ill for more than five years. I wasn't getting better. As the pastor of a large charismatic church, I believed in divine healing. Yet, I wasn't being healed—I was getting worse.

This book is about how to have the kind of faith that *really* works—all the time… every time. That was the kind of faith I desperately needed. You need it, too.

Life-saving Word

For many years, I had believed for my healing, but had not seen results. After years of trying to have faith, I had given up on being healed.

The combination of a serious heart condition and Type 2 diabetes had, according to my doctors, shortened my life expectancy by at least twenty years. It was so serious that one Sunday, prior to having heart surgery, I preached sitting on the edge of the platform, fearful that I might over-exert myself and trigger a heart attack.

I'm so very grateful that God had mercy and showed me how to have faith for my healing. As I write this chapter, God is performing a miracle in my body. Everyday, I'm being rid of my diseases. Under doctor's care, I'm using far less insulin than I once required and I believe God has given me a new heart. If He hadn't given me the truths in this book, I doubt I would be alive today.

This "word from the Lord" saved my life, and it can save yours. I believe that if you receive this message with an open mind and heart…you will not only discover what *real* faith is, you will know how to get it for any need you may have.

No "Word"

This teaching began when I discovered that I had nothing to preach for a particular Sunday service. I asked my associate pastor if he wanted to preach but, because he was giving a sermon series on Sunday evenings, he declined.

There was no sermon burning in my heart and that was extremely unusual. I *always* have something—or several things—to preach. Yet this time there was nothing.

By the Tuesday before I was to preach, I still had nothing to say and I knew there was a problem. When I got on my knees early that day, I didn't ask God for a sermon. I knew the sermon wasn't the issue. Rather I prayed, "God, *why* don't I have a word from You?" I knew the problem could only have one source—me.

I had no more than uttered those words when God spoke in my heart, "I gave you a message two months ago, but you don't want to preach it."

Instantly, I knew what He was talking about. God had given me a revelation on faith which I had mentally filed away for future use. However, I didn't want to teach it for what I considered to be two very good reasons.

First Reason—Walk the Talk

I didn't want to preach on faith because in some ways, I hadn't been living what God wanted me to say.

I was struggling with faith for my own healing. It wasn't that I had abandoned faith entirely. Like most Christians, I had strong faith in some areas and weak faith in others.

Faith for finances is my area of strength. Those who know me would say that I have "bulldog faith" for finances. I never fret or fear concerning money. During the summer months when churches typically go through a financial slump, I *know* God will provide…and He always does.

I accept as fact that the God Who owns the "cattle on a thousand hills" *and* the hills under their feet can easily provide the comparatively small amount necessary to meet our needs. Faith for the church or personal finances is no problem!

When it comes to the healing of *others*, I have great faith for certain illnesses and lesser faith for others. Over the years, God has healed many through my ministry.

Recently, while preaching, God told me that a lady in my church, who had been unable to conceive, would have a baby. Without hesitation, I told her and the entire congregation that she would receive this miracle—and she did.

Yet, faith for my own personal healing was another story. I must confess that I had abandoned all hope of ever being healed. In fact, I had made the statement that I couldn't get healed of a hangnail!

The Truth…the Whole Truth

If we are going to see an improvement in our faith, we must be honest about our faith failures, as well as our victories. In this book I have been transparent concerning my faith shortcomings because I'm convinced that if we will be genuine, change is possible.

We've *got to be* truthful about spiritual things. When our *apparent* faith doesn't work, we cannot be in denial, make excuses, or blame anyone else. If we hide from faith failures, we're unable to evaluate our faith or find out from God how to acquire the kind of faith we need to obtain miracles.

As I tried to look objectively at my lack of faith for personal healing, I recognized that I had had this weakness of faith for a long time.

Fruitless Faith

I recall waking up with a sore throat one morning, when I was just a young boy. I remember thinking, "I'll just ask Jesus to take that sore throat away."

So, I got on my knees and prayed for God to heal me. When I checked my throat—nothing had changed. I decided that I would stay on my knees until I got healed. I knelt there all day and finally gave up because my throat never improved.

As I analyze my lack of faith for personal health, I realize that this specific childhood experience had a negative impact on my ability to believe God for healing.

Decades later, as I stood behind the pulpit the day I taught this message to my congregation, I had a certainty in my heart that, despite my personal weakness, God expected me to teach on faith. Whether I was qualified or not—whether I was a faith success or failure in my own eyes—God would take the *truth about faith* and change lives.

Today, as I write this book, I have the same assurance in my heart that if you will receive this truth and put it into practice…it will change you, forever!

The Other Reason

Another reason I didn't want to begin this teaching on faith was because of the abuses of the faith message.

When I say "abuses," I recognize that some could be offended by that statement. Before you throw this book down, please understand—I'm totally convinced that faith is something the Body of Christ *must* have today. Yet, with all the wonderful truth we've received, I believe there have been some misunderstandings of Scripture.

I ask that you please hear me out with an open mind. "Chew on" the message in these pages, and if at the end it doesn't bear witness in your heart, "spit it out."

In some instances, I believe that faith teaching has become "carnal." By that I mean it has become for some like a "magic charm" to force God to give them what they want.

That approach to faith makes *us* lord of the universe and God an errand boy required to jump at our every command. I believe that, deep down, everyone knows there is something very wrong with that kind of belief.

A flawed faith message is devastating to *real* faith and has spiritually damaged many people. It has caused some to give up on "living by faith" and others to give up on God entirely. At best, this unsound belief is a naïve "head trip." At its worst, it is an attempt to control God based on the desires of the flesh.

Get Real!

I haven't had every prayer answered...have you? Yet, nowhere in the Bible did faith fail to produce a miracle! It stands to reason that if our faith isn't consistently producing miracles, something *is* amiss. I can't stress this truth enough!

Isn't it time for us to find out *why* our faith doesn't work all the time? Can we be honest enough to admit we may not have the whole truth about faith and ask God to reveal more? Personally, I didn't have a choice; I either had to get more revelation about faith or die before my time.

Faith "In"...Precedes Faith "For"

Faith is so important to our Christian lives; we can't afford to gamble with it spiritually. We must discover real faith, the kind that *always* produces results...so that we can receive healing for ourselves and our loved ones...and bring God's promises of blessing and prosperity into our lives.

In the Bible or through sermons we can *learn* Who God is, but only through our personal, intimate relationship with Him can we *know* Who He is and obtain *real* faith. We must believe "in" God—His nature and intentions toward us—before we can have faith "for" the things that He has promised.

The first principle of *real* faith: *You have to believe "in" God before you can believe Him "for" things.*

Oneness Creates Faith

My wife and I have been married for almost forty years. When you live with a person that long, in an intimate relationship, you get to know them well. I don't have to arise every morning, muster faith in our marriage, and confess, "My spouse will be faithful to me today." That is totally unnecessary because I *know* her—she is faithful.

Out of knowing her through our intimate relationship has come "faith" in whom she is. After decades of marriage, we know each other well. We know how the other will react in almost any situation. The Bible says that when people marry, "two become one." Our "oneness" has created faith in each other.

We can have oneness with God. Jesus prayed, *"...That they all may be ONE, as You, Father, are in Me, and I in You; that they also MAY BE ONE IN US..."* (John 17:21).

The intimate "oneness" with the Father that Jesus had when He walked the earth is the same kind of relationship we can have with God today. According to Jesus, it is the relationship we *should* have. I believe it is the relationship we *must* have if we are going to have *real* faith— and be able to trust Him with every situation.

Faith Teaching of Jesus

In Mark 11:22, Jesus said, *"Have faith in God."* You might ask, "What does that mean?" Jesus was saying, "Have faith in Who God is—His nature and His intentions toward you."

The first thing we must know about God's nature is that He is a "good God." All the time and in every way, He is good. It isn't His nature...it isn't even *possible* for Him...to be wicked, petty, spiteful, evil, or anything but good.

Yet, we can read in the Word that "God is good," sing it in church, or say it until we are blue in the face, but until we perceive Him as "good" through our relationship with Him, we don't *really know it.* Just as I know my wife's nature through our close relationship, we also must know God intimately to comprehend that He truly wants to be good to us and faithful to His Word.

No Greater Love

Another thing we must *know* about God is that He loves us like a good father loves his children. Out of that fatherly love comes His desire to bring good things into our lives. The Word says in Psalms 84:11, *"...No good thing will He withhold from those who walk uprightly."*

As a grandparent, I've learned so much about God's love. There are no words to describe how much I love my grandchildren. Every Sunday, I look forward to hearing them run down the hall into my office, excited to see their grandfather. Through my feelings for them, I can begin to understand God's love for us. There isn't any truly "good thing" within my power to accomplish, that I wouldn't do for them.

God feels the same way about you. God loves you and me so much that He "sent his only begotten Son" to die for our salvation so that we could return to a father and child relationship with Him.

Get God's Thoughts

We must learn to trust God's intentions toward us. In Jeremiah 29:11, God tells us His intent, *"For I know the thoughts that I think toward you, says the LORD, thoughts of peace, and not of evil, to give you a future and a hope."* God's thoughts toward you are loving. He wants you to have a wonderful life.

We also need to understand how God relates to us. Hebrews 11:6 says, *"...He is a rewarder of those who diligently seek Him."*

We must believe that God wants us to prosper financially and in every way. Psalms 35:27, *"...Let the LORD be magnified, Who has pleasure in the prosperity of his servant."*

Likewise, we must believe that God wants to heal us. In Exodus 15:26, God says, *"...I am the Lord who heals you."* God's many names in the Old Testament reveal Who He is. In this verse God named Himself, *Jehovah Rapha,* "the God who makes you whole and heals you."

First, last, and above all else, we must come to *know* that God is faithful. Faithfulness is part of His nature and He is faithful to perform His Word.

Just as I want the best for my children and grandchildren and love to see them happy, doing well, prospering, and living in health, our heavenly Father feels precisely the same way about each of us.

Proud Faith vs. Greedy Faith

Some people become prideful because they have faith in God, but would never consider exercising it *for* "things." They tend to look in a condescending way at people who want to have faith "for" God's promises. They believe their faith is deeper and purer than those who believe God "for."

What they don't realize is that when you really have faith *in* God, you can't help but have faith in His goodness, in His giving nature, in His faithfulness and love. Out of knowing God, you *naturally* grow into a faith for Him to meet your needs.

You can't stop with faith in God because God doesn't stop there. Nor does He want you to stop short of the good things He has for you. Those who claim faith *in* but not *for* God's promises actually have neither.

A New Understanding

Hebrews 11:6 says, *"But without faith it is impossible to please him...."* Have you ever wondered: why faith is so important to God? What about faith is so significant that He isn't pleased unless we have it?

I've discovered that the word *please* used in Hebrews 11:6, in the original Greek means "to gratify." When you insert "gratify" into this scripture it reads, "Without faith it is impossible to *gratify* God."

"Gratify" goes beyond God being glad for us. The word gratify speaks to a longing or deep desire being fulfilled. To be perfectly honest, we think that faith, when it works, brings "gratification" to us. So, how could it bring gratification to God?

In my search to understand God's gratification, I discovered that the root word for *please*, means to "come into agreement with." *This is the key!* God loves it when we come into agreement with Him because, when we do, we are saying, "Yes," to His plan for our lives and the things He has spoken over us.

Surely you know that even before God created heaven and earth, He

10

knew you would be born and created a detailed plan that would give you more than just a "good life." God's plan would use all the talents He gave you to live a "great life"—one that is rewarding and fulfilling.

"Walking in faith" then is simply coming into full agreement with the things that God has planned for us. This distinction is very important and will strengthen your faith. We no longer must try to have faith for what *we want*, but rather for what *He wants* for us. When we do faith God's way, He is gratified, and so are we.

Principle of *real* faith: *"Faith" is coming into agreement with God.*

Faith Isn't Mental—It's Spiritual

When faith is only a mental thing, all we have is "positive thinking." Positive thinking is good, but it is *not* faith and it will not produce miracles.

This is a place we've missed it: we've thought that we could build faith by convincing our minds of God's truth. We've believed that if we would *read* God's promises concerning our need, *recite* those promises, and *sing* them, we would build real faith. Some have even prayed the promises in an attempt to convince God to keep them.

Hearing the Word of God is central to our faith, but faith involves more than just the mind. Although we can bring our minds into agreement with truth, they don't have the capacity to produce faith because our minds belong to the "natural," or "flesh" man.

Faith is spiritual! The "flesh" cannot produce the spiritual substance of faith. First Corinthians 2:14 says, *"...The natural man does not receive the things of the Spirit...."*

To make matters worse, we are often more *flesh*-conscious than *spirit*-conscious. We tend to be more aware of our thoughts, feelings, and desires than of our spirits. In fact, the flesh openly opposes the *spiritual*.

Minding Our Faith

What are we to do? Is faith then too hard for us? Can we do nothing to develop our faith? What should we do about our minds?

Relax! God wouldn't ask the impossible of us. Faith is natural and normal for a Christian who is in relationship with Him.

In subsequent chapters, I'll answer some of these questions more fully, but for now I want to make clear that we are instructed to bring our minds, in fact all our flesh, under the control of our spirits. We are told to *"...Take captive every thought..."* (II Corinthians 10:5 NIV). To maintain our faith, we must train our minds—not to create faith, but to sustain it.

Experiencing Real Faith

Most Christians have experienced *real* faith but didn't know what it was. They may have thought it was just a positive emotion or good feeling.

Perhaps you've heard a sermon that touched your heart and you walked out of church knowing God was at work in your situation and would answer your prayers. That was *real* faith.

Maybe, after a powerful time of worship, you've had a sense of well-being and assurance that God really was in control of your life. That was *real* faith.

At one time or another, you may have experienced an unnatural calm, peace, and assurance—a *knowing* that God cares and is taking care of your needs. That "knowing" is *real* faith. It doesn't come from your mind; rather it is produced in your spirit.

Don't misunderstand, faith isn't based on a feeling. Yet, at times, faith *produces* feelings. The real question is—and we'll be dealing with it later—how was that *real* faith produced in our spirits?

Faith's Fortification

After experiencing *real* faith, we often allow both mind and emotions to focus on our circumstances. We are reminded of the "facts" and we lose our "knowing." We allow fear (our emotions) and reasoning (our minds) to rob us of our faith. God's Word will help us to defend our faith.

The Bible tells us in I Timothy 6:12 to *"Fight the good fight of faith...."*

That fight is in the area of our "flesh" and includes our minds. We must saturate our minds with God's Word... encourage ourselves with faith statements... and inform "natural" reasoning with God's truth. Scripture reading, confessions, and positive reminders protect our faith. Remember: these activities don't create faith, they nurture it.

Faith Actions

Faith is not passive but *active*—you will have to fight for your faith. Faith isn't just training your mind or waiting patiently for God to act— you need act on your faith.

Praise is a faith action. Take every opportunity to praise God, speak and sing your thanks to Him, and give glory to God for what you *know* He will do. It will reinforce your faith. The Bible says that Abraham, "...*was strengthened in faith, giving glory to God*" (Romans 4:20).

Another faith action is *being expectant*. Faith expects a miracle. Begin every morning thanking God that your miracle is "on the way."

If a relative called to say they had mailed you a large check, you would go to your mailbox every day *expecting* the money. You would know that it could come any day. In the same way, wake up each day expecting God's miracle provision to come into your life *that* day. Your attitude should be: if it doesn't come today, it could easily come tomorrow, but it will come. The important thing is that you *know* it is coming.

Although things couldn't have looked worse for Abraham—both he and his wife were well beyond childbearing age—he expected God to keep His promise. The Bible says that Abraham was "...*fully convinced that what* [God] *had promised, He was also able to perform.*"

In His Word, God has promised to do things for you, too. Don't give up on God or your faith in Him! A promise is only as good as the one who gives it. So, like Abraham, *your knowing* of the goodness and faithfulness of God is based on your relationship with Him.

Vanished Faith

After being sick for years, I honestly thought I would never be healed. One day as I was feeling sorry for myself, the Lord strongly rebuked me. He said, *"No! I don't want you to live like that. I want you to grab hold of that thing you once believed Me for. I want you to expect the manifestation of your healing. I want you to live every day in expectation."*

Have you let go of something you once believed God for—an unsaved loved one, a healing, or a financial provision? Have you prayed and believed for this situation for years, but never seen a change and now you're just tired of hanging on?

If you think your faith isn't working, I want to encourage you, "Don't give up!" There is a *real* faith…a faith that *always* produces miracles.

Real faith isn't hard. When you obtain it in the right way, it's as natural as breathing. You can do it because God has called and created you to walk in faith! As I write this book, faith is causing my body to be healed and it will work in your need, too. I *know* it!

CHAPTER 2

========================

A FAITH TO "LIVE" BY

I t was two weeks between the time I preached my first sermon on faith and the next one. Those were two weeks from hell for my family and me. During that time, the devil attacked with sickness my wife, children, grandkids, me, and even my dogs. I won't go into the grisly details. Let it suffice to say we all suffered.

I knew this was an attack on my faith by Satan. It was time to "put up or shut up," and hang onto the spark of faith God had put in me. I was determined to stand up to Satan and tell him what he could do with his sickness. You, too, *must* take a stand against the enemy's attacks, or he will walk over you.

I said to Satan, "I'm the healed, not the sick. I will not tolerate infirmity in my body, and I certainly will not tolerate it in my family!"

Paper Shield and Paring Knife Sword

I don't want you to get the wrong impression. Although I knew that I was carrying my shield of faith and wielding the sword of the Spirit, my shield felt like a paper cup and my sword seemed like a paring knife. When *you* take a faith stand, you may also feel weak and powerless...but do it anyway.

As I exercised my seemingly fragile faith, something amazing happened. Spiritual "life" began bubbling up in me. My small amount of faith began to grow. Life coursed through my body, and I started to sense victory.

This physical attack was no coincidence. It was a deliberate attempt of the enemy to steal my faith for healing. Actually, it was predictable. When *you* take a faith stand, you can expect to have your faith attacked, too.

Stolen Faith

Jesus' parable in Mark 4:15 explains Satan's number one method for defeating our faith—theft. He tried to use it on me and he will try it on you: *"And these are the ones by the wayside where the word is sown. When they hear, Satan comes immediately and takes away the word that was sown in their hearts."*

Satan knows that he must undermine your faith quickly, or you will receive your miracle. Somehow, he must persuade you that God didn't really speak to you, or has disqualified you from receiving a miracle.

He tries to steal your faith by turning your focus away from God's promise. Satan will try to distract you through some type of attack—and God will allow your faith to be tested.

That attack may be sickness, like it was for my family and me. You could have a challenge in your finances, at work, or in some other area. Satan will strike you where you're most vulnerable. He'll speak unbelief to your heart, and play on your fears. Often, he strikes in the very area where you are believing God for a miracle. If you're sick, he may make you sicker or give you a *bad report* on your illness.

I've got *good news!* You don't have to passively endure his assault. You can do something about it. James 4:7 says, *"...Resist the devil and he will flee from you."* Although he MUST flee, he will hang around for as long as he can. So you must "stand"—use your faith as a shield until he withdraws and leaves empty-handed.

Even if Satan has won some ground and you find yourself facedown in the mud, the fight isn't over. You may get knocked down, but you aren't out of the fight unless you "throw in the towel." You can get back up, knock out the devil, and reclaim your miracle in round two. Get up! Dust yourself off and take back what's been stolen!

The Fight of Faith

Walking in faith isn't a "cakewalk," but neither is it impossible. First Timothy 6:12 tells us to *"Fight the good fight of faith,...."* God knows that we are going to have to fight to keep our faith and has given us an example of real faith in Abraham.

"And not being weak in faith, he DID NOT CONSIDER his own body, already dead (since he was about a hundred years old), and the deadness of Sarah's womb. He DID NOT WAVER at the promise of God through unbelief, but was strengthened in faith, giving glory to God" (Romans 4:19, 20).

How did Abraham do it? Why, despite the seeming impossibility of the situation, didn't he "waver at the promise of God"? Abraham's faith was strong because it was built on his close relationship with God. James 2:23 tells us that Abraham *"...was called the friend of God."* Friendship is close personal relationship. Because of this relationship, Abraham *knew* God could and would fulfill His Word. That is the kind of certainty that we desire and need.

God wants to be your friend, too. Jesus said, *"No longer do I call you servants,...but I have called you friends..."* (John 15:15). If you are born again, the way has been opened for an intimate relationship with God. For a deeper relationship, start spending more time with Him. Just as you spend quality time getting to know the person you love—make a way to spend time with your Father. Talk to Him, listen to Him, praise Him for His goodness to you.

Sick...or Symptoms

The facts were all stacked *against* Abraham's miracle: He was almost a hundred years old and he had been impotent for years. Her entire married life, Sarah had never been able to get pregnant. Now she was beyond childbearing age. In "the natural," they had no way to conceive a child. Yet, Abraham *"...did not consider his own body, already dead... and the deadness of Sarah's womb"* (Romans 4:19).

Does the phrase, "He didn't consider" mean that Abraham lied to himself and others by denying his physical condition? I don't think so. Yet, some teach that acknowledging our problems is contrary to faith.

According to this teaching, to "not consider" the problem means to avoid saying we are sick, poor, or need God's help in some way.

I must admit, this has bothered me for years. During the time I was seriously ill, people would often inquire about my health. I wanted to answer positively and would say something like, "Bless God, if I were doing any better it would be illegal." Yet, I'd walk away thinking, "John, you're a lying dog."

Years ago, we went to a faith church where my wife attended a Bible study. Once, when she asked them to pray for our children who had been sick all week, they instructed her, "Don't say your children are 'sick.' Say they have 'symptoms.'"

Shortly after that, I was attending a Sunday school class at the same church when a woman requested prayer for her little girl, whom she said had suffered all week with "symptoms."

I happened to be sitting next to her and midway through the class, the little girl threw up all over me. Her mother was listening to the teacher so intently that she didn't notice. So, I leaned over, tapped her on the arm, and said, "Excuse me. Your baby just got her symptoms all over my suit."

It can be dangerous to deny our illnesses. If we have pain, perhaps we should see a doctor. I believe it is dishonest to be in denial, lie to others, and lie to ourselves. I asked God, "Do you expect us to lie about our circumstances and not acknowledge our pain? Is that what Abraham did when he "considered not"?

Exercising Your Mind

I received my answer when I looked closely at the word "considered" in the verse "Abraham *considered* not his own body." *Considered* is a Greek word made up of two words—a suffix and a prefix. When used separately each of the words has an individual meaning.

The second word or suffix means "to exercise the mind." If this word is plugged into the verse without the suffix, it causes the verse to mean what some have taught: "Abraham did not exercise his mind, but was strong in faith." Yet, that raises the question, "Why did God give us a mind if we aren't supposed to use it?"

The prefix, or first word, is where the complete truth comes out. When the two words are combined, the meaning becomes: "over and against, or in opposition to." The idea of "considered not" now has a whole new meaning. This scripture is really saying that Abraham "did not exercise his mind in opposition to his faith." In other words, he didn't allow his mind to oppose or negate his faith.

Denial Isn't Faith!

This is important! Abraham didn't deny the *fact* that Sarah and he were unable to have a child. Yet, neither did he allow these "natural" facts to overwhelm his faith.

Using our minds to understand our need is *not* a lack of faith. Yet, if we allow our minds to oppose our faith and battle our beliefs, we will destroy our faith.

Take my illness as an example. The doctors told me that my heart condition and diabetes were bad and getting worse. They said my condition would drastically shorten my life. Those were the "natural" facts.

Some might advise me to deny the "facts" of my illness and call them symptoms instead. I'm sorry to admit this, but it's the plain truth: if I had added denial to my lack of faith and avoided my doctors' advice, I'd probably be dead or incapacitated by now. *Denial of the truth isn't faith… it's fantasy.*

Until God taught me how to have *real* faith, the facts of my illness completely overwhelmed my fragile faith for healing. *You* don't have to make my mistake—like Abraham, you can recognize the facts, but resist the temptation to give in to hopelessness.

This truth can set you free to have *real* faith. God doesn't want you to act like the bad things aren't there. Faith is *real* and doesn't need to be supported by lies.

The Abraham kind of faith says: "I'm in pain, but I don't care that my body and doctor tell me I'm sick. I'm going to believe what God says—'I'm the healed!' My billfold is empty, the creditors are calling, and the taxman is knocking at my door. Yet, I choose to believe what God says—'I am the blessed!'"

Principle of *real* faith: *The faith of Abraham acknowledges the situation, but doesn't allow the mind to oppose faith.*

"Life" through Faith

Hebrews 10:38 says, *"Now the just shall live by faith; But if anyone draws back, My soul has no pleasure in him."* The phrase, "The just shall live by faith" must be important to God. He "underlined" it by repeating it two other times in the Bible.

Some have mistakenly believed this verse to mean that living by faith means a poor and meager existence, one step above destitution. This interpretation is in direct opposition to the rest of the Bible. The Scriptures are filled with verses that declare God's desire for us to *"...prosper in all things and be in health, just as* [our] *soul prospers"* (III John 2).

The real meaning of "The just shall live by faith" is this: *we obtain spiritual life through faith.* The word "live" in this verse is a form of the Greek word, *zoë*. This is the same word Jesus used when He declared, *"...I have come that they may have LIFE, and that they may have it more ABUNDANTLY"* (John 10:10).

Zoë life isn't a sparse meager way of life. No! It is the vigorous life of God...the power that raised Christ from the dead...the might of the Spirit of God living inside us.

Faith is the "delivery system" for the *zoë* life of God. Just as blood is vital to the health of our bodies because it carries oxygen, nutrients, and other needful things to our cells, faith is vital to our spiritual life. It carries the "life" of God to areas of need. Faith can revive your body or any "deadness" in your life.

Spiritually Dead

As a Christian, you weren't meant to live a mere *natural* life; you were meant to live *supernaturally.* If you are struggling in your spiritual life or feel that you are drying up and dying spiritually; or if you have never known a vital, exciting Christian life—then it's time to exercise your faith. Believe God to meet a need...look to Him in everything. This is "walking by faith."

When faith is *active* in your life, you are focused on the *super*natural life to which you are called. This supernatural life in Christ is possible only *through* faith. If you are merely believing "in" God, but not believing "for" your needs, you have severed your connection to the "abundant" life.

It is time to return to the belief that:

- God can do *anything*
- He loves you
- You can take any need to Him and He will meet it
- Your prayers are effective and avail much
- God is making a difference in your life.

Make a resolution not to let up and to believe that God will meet your *every* need.

Ridiculous Faith

Trying to be a Christian without having the "life" that comes through *real* faith doesn't work and can lead to a religion based on works, ritual, man-made formulas, and other errors.

A member of my church came to me one day to talk about an investment he was making. He was going to put everything he owned—millions!—into a ridiculous scheme.

Because I'm the kind of person who will tell you what I think if asked, I told him this project was a crazy idea. I asked him why he thought it would succeed. His answer was chilling. He said, "If I have enough faith, it doesn't matter what I do. Whether it's wise or not, God is obligated to bless me."

Do you see his error? He actually believed that he could do as he chose, apply a certain formula, and thereby compel God to bless his foolishness.

Formulas will never replace or produce faith. I told him that he would lose everything, and unfortunately he did—not only the millions he invested, but his home and everything he owned. He ended up filing for bankruptcy.

Faith isn't a head-trip…faith isn't a formula we "do" to manipulate God. *Real* faith brings "life" to our finances and everything it touches.

Christian Agnostics

People who once believed in faith and have since forsaken it have become what I call "Christian agnostics." They know God exists. They believe that He loved the world enough to send His Son to die on a cross for their sins. They believe that Jesus and His disciples did miracles. They even believe that they are born again.

They claim to believe God's Word, yet, in their hearts they don't embrace important truths. They don't believe that God cares very much about them personally or that He responds to their faith and works miracles today. Their God is far away, deaf to their prayers, and aloof. They certainly don't believe the scripture that says, *"Jesus Christ is the same yesterday, today, and forever"* (Hebrews 13:8). God has become a faded idea instead of a powerful reality in their lives.

If you have lost your belief in faith, then you have lost your belief in a good God, One Who really cares about you. You've forgotten that God has promised to answer prayer. Hebrews 11:6 says that God *"...is a rewarder of those who diligently seek Him."*

You may have drifted away from your relationship with God; or perhaps you've never had relationship, but only religion. You can return to what you once knew or find the supernatural life you always wanted—all you have to do is "seek Him."

From Death to LIFE

If you are born again and thinking that you have never successfully had faith for anything, let me remind you that you received salvation by faith. Faith for salvation caused the supernatural life of God to pour into your spirit and birthed it anew.

The way that you receive salvation is the same way you receive any of God's promises. Ephesians 2:8-10 describes what happened when you were born again: *"For by grace you have been SAVED THROUGH FAITH, and that not of yourselves; it is the gift of God, not of works, lest anyone should boast."*

Faith is something every Christian has. You can "do" faith because you've done it before. You can send *zoë* life to your dead situations. However, the supernatural, miracle-making "life" of God will only go

22

where your faith makes room for it to flow.

Principle of *real* faith: *Faith conveys the "abundant life" to dead situations and causes miracles.*

Discouraged Faith

Does it seem that you are losing your spiritual "edge"? Can you look back on a time when you were more excited about following Jesus? A time when God was doing things in your life? Those who give up on faith can never have the fullness of the incredible life God planned for them.

Christians who are not living by faith can only *hope* that God will "bless" their situations and their efforts to deal with problems. They must hope for a "sovereign act" of God to meet their needs. How it must grieve the heart of God to see His people live so far below the wonderful life He has planned for them.

If you are one who would say, "I've tried walking in faith, and it didn't work for me." I must tell you again that *real faith always produces a miracle!* When the "life" of God surges into a situation by faith, that circumstance *must* change—it has no other option. I don't think I can state strongly enough how important faith is to living a Christian life.

Faith Is a Must!

If you are thinking, "This chapter is talking about me and my life" and you would say, "To some extent, I've given up on faith. My life isn't an adventure with God, my spiritual life has slipped"…I understand you perfectly.

What you are reading in this chapter is what a desperate man learned while trying to get his faith restored and his spiritual life back on track. My spiritual and physical life would both have been wrecked if I hadn't found a faith that worked. I've discovered that I cannot "live" a vital Christian life without a strong faith…and neither can you.

You *can* get your spiritual life back on track and rediscover *real* faith! You can have a life so exciting, it will take your breath away and a faith so genuine it will move the hand of God to give you the miracle answers you need. The first step is so simple, you can do it right now...bow your head and pour out your heart to Him.

"Draw near to God and He will draw near to you....Humble yourselves in the sight of the Lord, and He will lift you up" (James 4:8, 10).

CHAPTER 3

━━━━━━━━━━━━━━━━━━

FAITH BEYOND HOPE

I preached the series of sermons that led to this book approximately every other week over a five-month period. Just preaching these sermons was a leap of faith for me. During the time between messages, the Lord would give me new insights about faith and show me how to practice them in my own life.

Through God's Eyes

As I learned about faith, I discovered that we often look at our situations and ourselves in a wrong way. We view them through the eyes of the flesh and form opinions based on what we see. Not only is this opposite of what God wants us to do, it is also harmful to our faith. God wants us to see things through *His* eyes.

For example, Ephesians 5:27 says that Jesus is returning for a *"...a glorious church, not having spot or wrinkle...holy and without blemish."* I've heard preachers say that if the Lord is coming for a "spotless Church," the Church had better clean up her act. That assessment comes from a narrow, "fleshly" view of God and His Church.

We need to come into agreement with what God says concerning the Church. The Bible declares, *"...God, who is rich in mercy,... made us alive together with Christ... and raised us up together, and made us sit together in the heavenly places... that in the ages to come He might show the exceeding riches of His grace in His kindness toward us in Christ Jesus"* (Ephesians 2:4-7).

Does that sound like God is frowning down from heaven saying, "When they get their act together, I'll rapture the Church…and not a minute sooner"? The world and flesh-minded Christians may never see the Church as perfect, but God sees it that way.

Superior Sight

When you look at the situations in your life what do you see? Be honest! Do you see sickness, financial problems, unsaved children who are making bad decisions, a marriage that is falling apart, and so on?

Take my sickness as an example. When I looked at my physical "state," I saw a sick and dying man. That was the fleshly viewpoint. However, when God looked at me, He saw a *well man* whom the devil was trying to kill with sickness. God sees you victorious in every situation you face in life.

To develop our faith, we must stop evaluating circumstances according to the eyes of our flesh. We need to find out what God says about our needs then come into agreement with His viewpoint. Remember, faith is coming into agreement with God's will.

When you come into agreement with God, believing what He says about your situation, you will loose His miracle power in your life. The Scriptures are clear—*real* faith moves the hand of God.

The Little Engine That Could?

One day as I studied Hebrews 11, the famous faith chapter, I began to look for "natural" explanations for the incidents mentioned there. I explored interpretations that would not reach the conclusion that faith moved the hand of God to produce a miracle.

First, I looked at Abraham's story. In obedience to God he left his home and went to another land. It seemed to me that faith hadn't moved God, it had moved Abraham. The same could be said of Noah. His faith in God's warning of a coming flood caused *him* to do something—build an ark.

As I continued through Hebrews chapter 11, I began to consider the possibility that faith was like the children's story *The Little Engine That*

Could. Is it possible that faith causes people to believe in themselves more and say, "I think I can. I think I can. I think I can"? Did their positive attitude cause them to accomplish marvelous things? In other words, is it possible that faith doesn't move the hand of God...it moves us to go beyond ourselves?

Proof Positive-Faith Causes Miracles

Then I came to Hebrews 11:29 which talks about the nation of Israel crossing the Red Sea as dry land...verse 30 where the walls of Jericho fell down...and verse 35 which says, *"Women received their dead raised to life again...."*

Neither a positive attitude nor superhuman effort will dry up a sea... knock down the walls of a fortified city... or raise the dead. That requires a miracle! I think that constitutes proof that *real* faith, as illustrated by the people of Hebrew 11, does move God to perform miracles.

Next, look at Peter's best-known miracle, the healing of the lame man at the gate of the temple (see Acts 3:1-8). After performing this miracle, the Sanhedrin interrogated Peter and asked him how he did it. Peter explained that this miracle was performed through faith in the name of Jesus. Again we find that faith moved the hand of God.

Lastly, look at what Jesus said in Mark 11:23, 24:

> *"For assuredly, I say to you, whoever says to this mountain, 'Be removed and be cast into the sea,' and does not doubt in his heart, but believes that those things he says will be done, he will have whatever he says. Therefore I say to you, whatever things you ask when you pray, believe that you receive them, and you will have them."*

This scripture makes it crystal clear, if you have *real* faith...you *will* move the hand of God and your prayer will be answered.

Those who claim to believe "in" God, but think it greedy to believe "for" things, *must* have a problem with this scripture. They would say, "God is sovereign and He doesn't have to do anything!" That's true, yet, this scripture makes it obvious that God *will* answer faith-filled prayers. "Whatever you ask...believe that you receive...and you will have." Why would Jesus state this faith principle so clearly if it were inappropriate or too difficult to apply?

When Faith Flounders

As I write this, I can almost hear some say, "Well, I know So-And-So trusted in God for their healing—and they died." I'm sure most people who read this book would say they stood in faith for something that didn't come to pass.

Having said that, we must stop and examine the statement, "I stood in faith and God didn't answer my prayer" because it suggests something very destructive to faith.

Neither can we make excuses for God when He doesn't seem to answer prayer. The idea that God only answers *some* prayers at *some* times will destroy your faith. It wounds our souls and weakens our faith for the next time we want to believe Him for something.

How can we have faith in a God Who isn't "faithful"...a God Who doesn't answer all our prayers? I've sought God concerning this and believe He has given me an answer.

"Mysteries" of the Kingdom

Some would say in their deep religious voice: "Well, there are just some things we don't understand," or "God moves in mysterious ways." Yet, since the time of Adam, God has attempted to communicate and be understood by us. It has never been His purpose to be mysterious; in fact, just the opposite is true. God wants a relationship with us built on an *understanding* of Who He is and our relationship—our kinship with Him.

Think about this: If God really wants us to "walk in faith," and if it is impossible to please Him without faith, why would He be inconsistent and hide the workings of faith from us? The question then of why some prayers go unanswered begs an answer, because it casts doubt upon *everything* we know and believe about God.

If we maintain that we were standing in faith and didn't get a miracle, then we must assume that God doesn't always keep His Word. We may not be aware of it but we are proposing that God is sometimes unfaithful—and that is unthinkable.

If God is capricious and inconsistent in answering prayer, how can we know for certain that our prayers for salvation were effective? Do you see why this is so important? Unanswered prayer strikes a blow at the very core of our belief regarding our salvation and the nature of God. Consequently, we have to *know* why our faith doesn't work at times. Is it Him…or is it us?

It Wasn't Real!

I assume you know there are prayers that God will never answer. In James 4:3 it says, *"You ask and do not receive, because you ask amiss, that you may spend it on your pleasures."* If you've been praying for God to give you the winning numbers for the lottery, save your breath.

God does not answer prayers that merely indulge our fleshly appetites. This book is not about those types of faith failures. It *is* about understanding why we sometimes fail to receive what God has already promised in His Word.

I recognize that some people hate to think a faith failure was their fault. Many people are sold on their faith formula and unwilling to question it. Some fear that they would destroy their faith if they question their faith beliefs. They've come to believe that faith in their formula is the same as faith in God. Despite disappointment and lack of results, they cling to a failed formula in which they really may no longer believe.

Although it hasn't worked for them and they may doubt the faith formula or distrust their ability to practice it, still they cling to it. They pretend to believe in it for fear of losing *any chance* of receiving from God. They would rather blame a failure on God than find fault with their way of believing. Yet, the only sane conclusion we can draw when we fail to receive from God is that we weren't standing in *real* faith at all.

After thirty-eight years of pastoring, I've come to the conclusion that *real* faith is extremely rare in the Church. What is more common is *hope* miscalled *faith*. *Real* faith is not impossible or even hard to do. I think it is simply misunderstood by many.

Dear reader, someone can teach you how to "speak" faith…say all the right words and quote powerful scriptures…and you can declare truths until you run out of breath. Yet, you can still remain rooted in doubt and unbelief. Doesn't the fact that someone has to teach us what to say and do prove we're in doubt and unbelief? I suspect that what many have thought was faith was merely hope.

Hope Hopes…Faith Knows

What is the difference between faith and hope? It is simple. Hope can only wish that God would answer prayer, whereas *real* faith *knows* God will provide a miracle. There is a huge gap between the two.

Although it isn't *faith*, hope is a good thing. Psalm 31:24 declares, *"Be of good courage, and He shall strengthen your heart, all you who hope in the LORD."* Psalm 33:18 adds, *"Behold, the eye of the LORD is on those who fear Him, on those who hope in His mercy."*

I especially like Psalm 43:5, *"Why are you cast down, O my soul? And why are you disquieted within me? Hope in God; for I shall yet praise Him, the help of my countenance and my God."* Hope is important to believers, yet it cannot replace faith, build faith, or give you a miracle.

Hope Gone Bad

There is a dark side to hope. Proverbs 13:12 warns, *"Hope deferred makes the heart sick…."* This is exactly what has happened to many good Christian people who at one time loved the Lord but have drifted away. Think about that!

Prayers that were merely hope never produced results and caused disappointment or "heart sickness" that may have been the source of a decline in your spiritual life or in someone you know. When the faith formula fails to get results, it will make you sick at heart.

The Hebrew language is a pictorial language, and the word *sick* in the above scripture literally means "to wear sore."

It's like this: you purchase a new pair of hiking boots and head to the mountains to try them out. You quickly notice that something is wrong with the heel of the boot, but you go ahead and hike anyway. With each step, your boots chafe your feet until they "wear a sore" in the flesh. Instead of helping you scale the mountain, your boots have caused painful blisters and a failed mission. They were the wrong boots.

That is how hope deferred makes the heart sick. You had hope and thought it was faith. When your prayer went unanswered, it made you spiritually sore, and the next mountain got bigger and harder to climb or perhaps you gave up entirely.

Standing in Presumption

Why does faith produce a miracle while hope fails? The reason is...hope doesn't require God's input or a relationship with Him. You can hope to win the lottery...get the mansion on the hill...or receive God's promises and the result will be the same—disappointment.

Hope is all about what we want and has little to do with what God wants. We can hope for any old thing. *Real* faith, on the other hand, requires a *rhema word* from God. The moment God gives you a rhema word concerning your need, His integrity is on the line. If you put your faith in that word and don't allow anything to cause you to give up, you *will* get what God promised 100% if the time.

If you claim to have stood in faith, but have failed to get an answer to prayer, you must reevaluate your claim. A failure of faith boils down to only two possibilities: either God is a liar Who doesn't keep His Word (and we definitely don't want to go there) or you were standing, not in *real* faith, but in presumption.

Principle of *real* faith: *Hope is mental not spiritual, doesn't require relationship or input from God, and can never become real faith.*

Your "Word" from God

Real faith *"...comes by hearing, and hearing by the word of God"* (Romans 10:17). Hearing God speak to us gives birth to faith. *Real* faith comes through hearing a personal *rhema word* from God concerning your need. The word *rhema* means "a PRESENT spoken word of God." You can't pick any old promise out of the Bible and apply it to your situation. It must be a *specific word* God speaks to *you*.

Every *rhema* word God speaks to you will contradict the natural world—the "facts" you know about your need. If you are sick, God will not say, "You're really *sick*." You already know that. What would be the point? Instead, God might say, "I am your healer; you are the healed." If you have financial needs, God will not tell you that you are *poor* and *needy*. Rather, He will say something like, "I am your supply; you are the prosperous."

A *rhema truth* shouldn't be confused with the thousands of promises found in God's Word. Romans 10:17 doesn't say that "faith cometh" by reading…quoting…singing…memorizing or meditating God's Word.

If faith came by those actions, we wouldn't need a relationship with God to get our prayers answered. If all we had to do was open the Bible, find a scripture, and repeat it to have faith, every Christian would be as rich as Bill Gates and live to be as old as Methuselah.

Principle of *real* faith: *Faith comes through a personal, specific, present-spoken word by God—a rhema word.*

A Frog's Faith

In the last chapter, we talked about salvation faith. I want to add another point about that. Some think that we simply decide to trust God for salvation. Yet, nothing could be further from the truth. Before being saved, we were like frogs sitting in a slimy pond.

Do you think a frog sitting in slime thinks, "I want to be a prince. I'm just going to believe for God to send along a beautiful girl to kiss me, and I'll turn into a handsome prince"? A frog is a frog and a sinner is a sinner. Frogs were born in slime and they love it. It's their instinct to be in slime. They don't want anything else.

We were born in sin; we had the instincts of sinners, and no desire to be anything else. Then one day, God in His mercy and grace reached out His hand and began to move in our hearts by the Holy Spirit. He showed us a wonderful life beyond the slime pond and deposited within us the *belief* that we could become "new creatures" in Christ.

That is what the Bible means where it says, "*…By grace you have been saved…*" (Ephesians 2:5). Even the faith we had for salvation wasn't something we cooked up…prayed up…or conjured up within ourselves—it was imparted through a *rhema* word we received for salvation. All we can take credit for is being bright enough to know a good thing when we saw it and smart enough to act on the faith God gave us.

Finding Your Rhema Word

Somehow, we've forgotten the faith lesson of our salvation. We've thought that the rules for faith have changed, and believed that we could produce faith by our actions. It doesn't work because all we can "work up" is hope.

I've tried the faith formulas. I know what it's like to guard every word for fear that saying the wrong thing would negate my healing. That approach to faith brings bondage. It is a work of the flesh. What we need is a *rhema* word from God for our situation. So one day, I asked the Lord for a *rhema* word. I said, "I want You to tell me, 'As of today you are healed of diabetes.'"

When I asked God for a rhema word, He spoke, but He didn't say what I wanted to hear. I won't say that God never gives the exact *rhema* word you want, but it hasn't worked that way for me.

The *rhema* word God gave me for my healing was, "I will satisfy you with long life" (see Psalm 91:16). That was definitely *not* what I expected or wanted to hear. My first reaction was, "Are You going to keep me alive but sick for the next twenty years? Will I be wishing every day that I were dead? Is this some kind of punishment?"

For months, I argued with God, trying to get Him to be sensible. I said things like, "God! You've got to take care of these problems in my body because I don't see how You can satisfy me with long life if You don't." You know how God is. He speaks and that's all He'll say on the subject.

I argued with Him until I was hoarse, and received no response. I had asked for a *rhema* word and I got it. Now it was up to me to believe and act upon it—or forget it.

The Next Step

I was far too desperate to let go of the word God had given and He obviously wasn't going to change it, so I caved in and said, "Okay Lord, I give up. I come into agreement with what You've said."

Perhaps you can imagine what a step of faith it was for me to stand before my congregation the next Sunday and announce this *rhema* word.

I'd kept my congregation informed as my health condition grew more acute. They didn't know all the particulars, but they knew my life was seriously threatened and could be drastically shortened by my illnesses. They knew my heart disease was serious enough that I could be walking down Main Street one minute and walking heaven's streets the next.

So when I stood in my pulpit before thousands of people and declared, "God has promised to satisfy me with long life," they were surprised and encouraged! God's *rhema* word had created enough faith in my heart that I could stand before my congregation and declare it.

As I came to terms with my promise from God, I realized that God was right, I did want more than healing. What I really wanted was a long and healthy life. If God had done it my way, He might have healed me one day and the next day a truck could have hit me.

So, of course, God's *rhema* word was better than what I would have chosen. Although you may not recognize it at first, that will be the case with *your* word, too. His answer is always better than what we think we want.

Once I lined up my thinking with God's *rhema* word and received it with joy and thanksgiving, I came back to God and said, "I am in total agreement. I *will* live and not die and be satisfied with long life, but Lord, we've still got a problem to deal with here." Then God gave me another *rhema* word.

An Important Point

I will tell you in the next chapter about my next "words." However, first I must make a critically important point: you have to embrace the word God gives you regardless of what it is, because God really *is* sovereign.

Don't make the mistake of thinking that God doesn't want to heal, prosper, or meet the needs of some people. That is bunk. There are too many places in the Bible where God declares Himself to be our healer and provider. Yet, because God is sovereign, He will always do it *His* way, not ours.

So, the process for me to obtain my healing or for you to get your miracle is the same:

- Desire in your heart to be in relationship with God.

- Ask for and become content with the *rhema* word you get.

- Come into agreement with *everything* God tells you whether you like it or not.

When you approach faith this way, with God calling the shots, He will give you revelation after revelation to bring you into the fullness of your miracle.

Real faith begins when the sovereign God gives guidance through a "word." Then you establish faith in your heart by coming into agreement with Him and basing your faith on His personal word for your situation. This is the surefire way to get your miracle.

Waiters Are Winners

Isaiah 40:31 takes on new meaning with our deeper understanding of *real* faith: *"But those who wait on the LORD shall renew their strength; they shall mount up with wings like eagles, they shall run and not be weary, they shall walk and not faint."* Those who "wait," spend time with God, and receive their *rhema word* are the ones who receive their miracles.

God will not be a puppet on a string controlled by our idea of faith— He will direct our miracle or it won't happen. We don't look to a for- mula, rather we are *"...looking unto Jesus,..."* allowing Him to be *"...the author and finisher of our faith..."* (Hebrews 12:29).

CHAPTER 4

THE RIDDLE OF FAITH

I 've been sharing with you a journey of faith that started more than a year before I sat down to write this book and continues to this day. Each faith principle set down in these pages was a discovery tested in the laboratory of my life.

Much of what happened to me is deeply personal-particularly the events recounted in this chapter. Yet, this truth is so exciting; I can't wait to share it. It literally changed my life, and I believe that if you will receive it and allow it to work in you, you'll be changed, too.

Hearing God's Voice

Some who read this book may think that the kind of faith, which depends on hearing a "word" from God, is impossible for them. Perhaps you think God never speaks to you or if He does, you can't hear Him. If you truly desire to hear from God, the first thing you must do is to stop telling yourself that you *can't* hear Him.

This isn't positive thinking, it's agreeing with the Word of God in John 10:27 that says, *"My sheep hear My voice, and I know them, and they follow Me."* If you are one of God's sheep, He *does* speak to you. That should settle the issue and you can begin confessing that you *do* hear from God.

When God speaks to you, His first priority is usually your *spiritual* health. Third John 2 says, *"Beloved, I pray that you may prosper in all things and be in health, JUST AS YOUR SOUL PROSPERS."* God wants your soul to prosper first. You will also find that God often speaks to you about root causes of your problems rather than the problem itself.

If you're sick and have unforgiveness in your heart, God will probably speak to you about forgiving *before* He talks to you about healing. If you have sin in your life and you are seeking Him for prosperity, He will probably talk to you about turning away from a sinful lifestyle *first*.

After you have dealt with the issues God considers *most* important, He *will* speak to you about what you consider to be pressing concerns. I believe that many people *do* hear God speak, but dismiss His words because they don't believe God would say such a thing and think it's the devil, don't like what they hear, or consider it unrelated to their need.

As you will discover in this chapter, God often says things you don't expect or want to believe. I wonder how many people have gotten a precious "word" from God, the answer for their need, but dismissed it as a crazy irrelevant thought.

A Crazy "Word"

How can you know when you've heard from God and not from your mind, feelings, or even the enemy? Let me share something that has helped me to know when I've heard a *rhema* word.

When God speaks to me, His message often sounds "off the subject" and almost always sounds ridiculous. I'm not joking! Often, when He speaks to me, my reaction is "That is craziness! It's the wildest thing I've ever heard. It makes no sense at all."

That kind of response is almost a guarantee that I have heard from God. First Corinthians 2:14 says, *"...The natural man does not receive the things of the Spirit of God, for they are foolishness to him; nor can he know them, because they are spiritually discerned."*

As we've discussed previously, our mind is not born again; it is part of our "natural man." Consequently, our mind's first reaction to spiritual truth is to see it as "foolishness."

When I hear something in my spirit that I *know* I could never have thought up, something that doesn't make sense to me—it is probably from God. Of course, it can't be contrary to His Word. On the other hand, if what I hear sounds sensible, I know that I probably came up with it myself. When I hear a *rhema* word, a period of internal debate and sometimes even arguing with God is required before I can get beyond the stage of thinking it is "foolishness" and get to the level of "spiritual discernment."

My Journey of Faith

Over the years, I've asked God to show me *why* I can have "great faith" for finances yet not enough faith to heal a hangnail. This question has frustrated me for decades. I finally got the answer…it's powerful…and if you are struggling with faith in some area, it could be for you, too.

As my physical condition worsened, I prayed, "God, look down on Your servant. I have served You to the best of my ability. I'm trying to lead Your people in the things of the Lord. Yet, my sickness is an embarrassment to me—and it must be to You, too."

Sometime after that, I received the first *rhema* word from God: "I will satisfy you with long life." I've told you already that this was not what I wanted to hear and it made no sense to me. In fact, this "word" confused me. Every day was a struggle just to exist; yet God was saying that He would keep me alive for a *long* time. It didn't sound like a good thing; it sounded more like torture.

As I recount my conversations with God in this chapter and throughout the book, you may find it strange that a man who has been a Christian all his life, and a pastor most of his adult years, would speak so candidly with God. I figured out a long time ago that pious sounding words neither fool nor impress God. Since the Bible says that God knows the thoughts of my heart, I've decided I may as well be honest.

After all, I want God to be honest with me. When you read David's psalms, you'll find that many of his conversations with God were frank, honest, and emotional exclamations from his heart. God appreciates it when we get *real* with Him, and you'll find that it's a lot easier to pray when you are being *sincere*.

As I told you in the previous chapter, I finally came into agreement with God and decided to receive that "word." When I said with sincerity,

"Yes. I'll receive Your 'word' for me," I began to feel the life of God bubble up on the inside. Then I knew for certain that I *had* heard from God.

For months, I continued to confess my *rhema* word, "God is going to satisfy me with long life"…and *nothing* happened. There was *no* physical change. I was truly convinced that I would live my whole "long life" sick. After I announced this "word" to my congregation, I was tormented with thoughts like, "You're going to die and all those people will think you were a fake." My faith in that *rhema* word was being tried, but I hung on to it.

Several months after receiving that "word," I awoke one morning to find my hands swollen and painful; they were so huge, I couldn't get my wedding ring off, and people noticed them. I went to the doctor and he ran exhaustive blood tests.

When I returned a week later, I was unprepared for the diagnosis. It was one of the most shocking things I had ever heard. It was every bit as devastating as when they told me I needed open-heart surgery.

The doctor looked at me very gravely and said, "I hate to tell you this, but you've tested positive for lupus." I was speechless. I didn't know what to say or do. He continued, "It *is* possible to test false-positive for lupus because of a reaction to medication. So, we're going to change your prescriptions. If the medications are causing your condition, you should get better in six to eight weeks."

Six weeks went by and I wasn't better. By the time eight weeks had passed, I was worse and the doctor positively diagnosed me with lupus. I was stunned!

Missing Your "Word"

Had I responded with a rote, charismatic faith statement like, "I'm just not going to receive that—I'm healed!" I doubt that I would have gotten the *next* "word" God had for me.

If I had *only* confessed healing without a personal "word" from God concerning my latest health problem, I would not have had the *real* faith required to deal with lupus. When I got on my face before God, I was not only very serious, I was beginning to be angry with Him. After all, God had told me that He would satisfy me with long life. I'd received it and confessed it—and now this new challenge had popped up.

I was in excruciating pain, twenty-four hours a day, seven days a week. It hurt so badly, I'd awaken in the middle of the night and grab my arms with all my might to try to relieve the pain. I cried out to Him, "God! I *must* have a word from You about the healing of my body."

My Darkest Hour

In my pain, anger, and despair, I said, "I don't want You to satisfy me with long life, if I have to live like this." Then God gave me another *rhema word*. He said, "It's okay to say that you are healed." Again I thought, "I don't want to hear this. It's crazy!"

This "word" was a particular problem for me because, as I said before, I've always been disturbed when people say, "Bless God. I am the healed," while they are obviously *still* sick. I've wanted to say back to them, "Be quiet! You're a reproach to the name of Jesus." It seemed to me that was a bold-faced lie based on denial.

So, I said to God, "Why do You tell me things that make no sense to me? You know it bothers me to say, 'I'm the healed' when I'm actually sick. If You want me to say, 'I'm healed' then heal me, and I'll say it." It does no good to argue with God; He never argues back. Reluctantly, I relented and unwillingly said, "Okay, I'm the healed. *There* I said it, but I *don't* believe it."

You can say anything you like, but if it doesn't come from your heart, your words are wasted breath. They will not activate the power of God in your life. While I was still arguing with God about saying I was the healed, He gave me *another* "word" that was even more distressing. He told me, "You are as healed as you are saved."

For days, I wondered about my salvation because it was obvious I wasn't healed. Then the Lord steered me back on track with, "I didn't say that you are as *saved* as you are healed, but that you are as *healed* as you are saved." This statement left me in a great quandary for several weeks, because I knew I was saved, but I clearly was not healed.

Puzzling the Pieces

During this time, I preached on Abraham's faith from Romans 4:19, *"...Being not weak in faith, he considered not his own body..."* (KJV).

I had discovered that the word *considered* doesn't mean that Abraham didn't acknowledge the aged condition of his and Sarah's bodies, as some would have us believe. As you'll recall from a previous chapter, we learned that *considered not* actually means that Abraham didn't "allow the recognition of his condition to overrule or defeat his faith."

After I preached that message, I felt like a man with four pieces to a puzzle and no clue how they fit together. Here's what I had to work with: One—God would satisfy me with long life. Two—it was okay to say that I was healed. Three—I am as healed as I am saved. Four—Abraham considered not his own body.

As I sat and meditated on all of this, I told God, "I've got to have some answers. My body is wracked with pain and I don't have a clue what You're trying to tell me." Suddenly, the blinders fell from my eyes and *I knew the answer!* Finally, at long last, I understood *why* I could have *real* faith for finances, but couldn't get a hangnail healed.

A Simple Solution

It was so simple. You may read it and wonder how a man who knows his Bible could be so dumb. Yet, if you were raised as I was, in a legalistic church, you may understand.

As a boy, I never knew if I was saved. I always *hoped* that I was. I was taught that every time I sinned, I was in the same class as the rankest of sinners—and going straight to hell. If you have lived with that kind of belief, you know it's no way to exist.

God revealed the truth about salvation to me through His written Word and by a *rhema* word. The word God made real to me was, "You are not saved by works of righteousness, but by His grace alone. You are saved by grace through faith" (see Ephesians 2:8, 9).

God taught me that I am saved even when I do things I shouldn't...speak things I shouldn't...and think things I shouldn't. I need to repent of those mistakes, but they don't change my identity as a saved person. Romans 8:16 says, *"The Spirit Himself bears witness with our spirit that we are children of God."* I know in my heart that I'm saved.

Faith Identity

Most pastors don't earn a lot of money. The average senior pastor in our country receives less than $40,000 a year and has a church of about 250 people. My salary is considerably more, but my church is about 20 times larger than average.

However, I remember pastoring and making $35 a week. My spiritual identity then was the same as it is now—I am blessed of God. Although my circumstances over the years have come into line with God's words, my identity has remained the same.

Long ago now, God revealed through His written Word and a *rhema* word that I am highly favored and blessed. I *knew* that was true regardless of the amount of money in my pocket. Instead of looking at the natural evidence that said I was poor, I believed what God said about me.

Yet, when it came to healing, I believed the opposite: I saw myself as a sick man trying to get healed. My identity for finances was founded on God's Word, but my identity for health was founded on my physical pain and the doctor's report.

I had allowed the doctor's "word" on my health to reign as a higher truth than God's Word, and then wondered why I couldn't get healed. Remember, faith is coming into agreement with God.

Whose Report?

Isaiah 53:1 says, *"Who has believed our report?...."* I had believed God's report concerning my salvation, but not concerning my healing. I believed the doctor's report and the voice of my pain. My doctor had said that the lupus *could* go away, but as far as I was concerned—I had it and it had me.

Let's look at Isaiah 53:1-3, the basis for my revelation:

> *Who has believed our report? And to whom has the arm of the LORD been revealed? For He shall grow up before Him as a tender plant, and as a root out of dry ground....And we hid, as it were, our faces from Him; He was despised, and WE DID NOT ESTEEM HIM.*

I was surprised to discover that this scripture was talking about *me*! I didn't esteem Jesus as my healer. I couldn't see that He had *already* taken away my sickness.

Principle of *real* faith: *You have to believe God's report and "esteem" Jesus as the provider for your need.*

Isaiah 53:4 goes on to say, *"Surely He has BORNE OUR GRIEFS and carried our sorrows; yet we esteemed Him stricken, smitten by God, and afflicted."* The word *griefs* in the Hebrew means "maladies, calamities." It is translated elsewhere "disease, grief, and sickness." The root word for *grief* in Hebrew means "to be weak, sick, afflicted, or to make sick."

The word *borne* is a verb meaning "to lift up and carry off." It is used 640 times in the Old Testament, and *every time* it refers to something being picked up and carried away. This scripture tells us that our sicknesses were taken from us, put on Jesus, and carried away by Him. I discovered that I could no longer say, "I'm a sick man who needs to be healed." My identity *must be* that I *have* perfect health, because God's Word says my sicknesses *were* taken from me!

Skip now to Isaiah 53:12, *"…He poured out His soul unto death, and He was numbered with the transgressors, and He BORE THE SIN OF MANY, and made intercession for the transgressors."* Again we find that Jesus "bore" something for us. The word for "bore" is the identical Hebrew word used in Isaiah 53:4 where it says He has *borne* our diseases.

So, Jesus also carried away our sins. We are the righteousness of God because all our sins were placed on Jesus and He carried them away to the Cross.

Finally, I got it! It's okay to say, "I am the healed," because Jesus has *already carried my sickness away*. In fact, He carried away *both* my sins and my sickness. So, "I'm as healed as I am saved!" I must tell you that this revelation makes it possible for me *and you* to say, "I am a person who walks in perfect, divine health."

Principle of *real* faith: *Your sicknesses, like your sins, were carried way by Jesus at Calvary.*

Divine health is ours *right now!* We don't plead with God to have mercy on us and wait for Him to take away our disease. In fact, He's waiting for us to claim the health and healing He has already made possible. Regardless of your diagnosis or when it was made, you are the healed because 2,000 years ago Jesus took that very disease away.

What About My Disease?

Some might ask, "Pastor John, what about the heart disease, the diabetes, and the lupus?" Let me tell you about the lupus. After receiving this truth, believing it…and applying it to my body, it wasn't long before I went back to the doctor and asked him to run those blood tests again.

This time his report came back: "No trace of lupus." The pain and swelling were completely gone. I was able to sleep through the night without pain. I could even play golf again. That's not all—I had to reduce my insulin injections because my "regular" dose was too high.

Some might say, "Yeah, but you still have a heart problem and you could die at any moment." NO! I'll tell you who has a *real* problem— Satan! He is trying to place himself and his sickness above the unbreakable Word of the Living God in my life and it won't work any more. I'm not buying it and neither should you.

Satan is trying to make sickness come into the body of a man who has been redeemed from sickness. Something has risen up inside of me and will no longer tolerate Satan's sickness in my body. This is not a faith formula confession…it's a *real* conviction.

As faith rose up within me, I could again feel the life of God flooding into my body. I have finally come into agreement with God, and sickness doesn't stand a chance in my body. It has no choice but to leave. Your negative situation, too, is a violation of God's Word concerning your identity. It has no right to remain—and it must go.

Not long ago, my wife said to me, "I feel like I'm married to a new man. You've never talked like this before."

Trickle-Down Blessing

I believe that as the patriarch "goes," so goes his family. I have three grown children, one son and two daughters. I have observed my son's wife give birth. She is very proficient at producing babies. It took her nine months of pregnancy and only forty-five minutes of labor to bear a beautiful baby.

My own daughters have suffered severely during childbirth. My oldest daughter was in hard labor for thirty-six hours for one of their children. It was so bad that finally, they had to rush her into surgery for an emergency c-section, because the baby's heartbeat was fading. My youngest daughter was in hard labor for twenty-six hours before giving birth to her first child.

Not long after I received my *faith realization*, we were driving to Denver for the birth of my youngest daughter's third child. During the drive, something welled up inside and I turned to my wife and said, "This one's going to be different. We have been redeemed from the curse and the blessing of God is on our lives."

Soon after we arrived at the hospital, the doctor checked my daughter, and because she had dilated to only four centimeters, he left to return to his office. He promised to check back at noon. If she hadn't started labor, he said that he would induce it. Shortly after he left, my daughter told us that something was happening. When the nurse examined her, she found that in twenty minutes my daughter had dilated to ten centimeters. She asked my daughter *not* to "push," but to wait for the doctor.

The nurse quickly called the doctor, and he had to turn around and come back to the hospital. When he arrived, he told my daughter to go ahead and push. With three "pushes," the baby was born. It was so easy, she wasn't aware that she had delivered her child.

Identity in the Word

I have loosed God's healing power in my body and in my family because I've come into agreement with what God says about me. I've chosen to assume my *real* identity—the healed—and you can do the same thing.

When you were born, your personal identity was imprinted on your genes and formed through your cultural and family heritage. When you were born *again*, God gave you a *new identity*. He stamped you with the seal of the Holy Spirit and forged your new personal identity

46

in Jesus—His death on the Cross and Resurrection to life. You are *far* more than you once were. You can now live above the curse of sin, sickness, poverty, and any other thing the devil might bring against you.

You were born (again) to be blessed…in every area of life. God identifies you as the head and not the tail, above and not beneath, the prosperous and not the poor, the forgiven and *not* the condemned, the well and *not* the sick, the delivered and *not* the addicted. Your "identity" in Christ makes every promise in the Book your birthright…through *real* faith.

CHAPTER 5

"I AM" FAITH

For Christians, faith is everything—the amount of victory you have in life is directly proportional to the amount of faith in which you operate. First John 5:4 says, *"For whatever is born of God overcomes the world. And this is the victory that has overcome the world—our FAITH."* To live the overcoming life the Bible says, *"…The just SHALL live by faith"* (Romans 1:17).

Faith Brush-up

I want to remind you that faith is vitally important. You must carefully guard it against attack by Satan…and by your unregenerate mind and emotions.

I know what it's like to allow Satan to steal your faith and not be in faith for anything. It is an awful way to live and it leaves you at the mercy of a merciless devil.

If God is not involved in your everyday life—if you don't see Him working in your situations—then you may have "head knowledge," but not a "working knowledge" of the victorious life God has provided. The solution is to get a new revelation of faith and allow God to work in your life.

You will be amazed at the change when you begin to *truly* live by faith. Since I received God's faith revelation for my health and began *acting* on it, I've had people tell me, "Pastor, you look ten years younger."

Easier Faith

In this chapter I want to consider how I got from where I was...living as a sick and dying man... to where I am today...a man who is seeing God's healing power at work in his body.

I've told you about the series of *rhema* words I received from God for healing and how I had to work past my foolishness to come into agreement with what God was saying to me. What I haven't mentioned is that I found the first *rhema* word, "I will satisfy you with long life," *far easier* to receive than those that followed. I've pondered why that might be and I think the answer is critical to our understanding of *real* faith.

Now or Never!

The reason I could more readily receive my first "word" from God is that it wasn't something I had to believe or lay claim to *immediately*. It was about a time to come: "I WILL (future tense) satisfy you with long life." The second and third "words" from God were different: "You can say that you ARE (present tense) the healed" and "You ARE (present tense) as healed as you are saved."

The present tense *rhema* words were the most difficult to accept because I was injecting insulin into my side three times a day. Every day, I could feel the sickness in my body and I thought, "It isn't possible for me to say that I am the healed *today*." I had lived with sickness for so long that my physical state, rather than the Word of the living God, determined my identity.

As I've told you, I thought of myself as a sick man trying to get healed. Before I could accept God's *rhema* words and begin to receive healing, I had to understand that God wanted to give me a very different identity—an "I am" faith identity. Despite the fact that sickness was rampant in my body, God was challenging me to believe His reality—a reality contrary to all physical evidence.

Real faith is never in the future tense; it *must be* in the present tense. In fact, faith for a future miracle isn't faith at all, but merely hope. With faith, it's now or never! That's why Hebrews 11:1 says, *"Now faith is the SUBSTANCE of things hoped for, the EVIDENCE of things not seen."* The word *substance* refers to something in the *present*. The expression *things hoped for* refers to the future. The word *evidence* means proof of a *present* truth. So when we give voice to our faith it must say, "I am healed, prosperous, delivered—NOW"!

God didn't tell me that I would *someday* be "the healed," or that sometime in the future I would be as healed as I am saved. That isn't *real* faith and it would never bring any of His promises into my life.

Real faith is taking hold of a truth that you can't see with your eyes, feel with your body, or prove in the natural world. "I am" faith sees the situation the way God sees it...solely because He declared it to be so.

Principle of *real* faith: *Effective faith is always in the present tense; otherwise it is without substance.*

Scriptural Verification

When you make a genuine faith declaration, your flesh and circumstances will tell you that you are crazy. When I decided to accept God's reality, my mind shouted, "You will be an embarrassment to God and your church. What you are saying isn't even true."

To have *real* faith for your situation, you will have to take a stand against *natural* facts. You must decide that the truth in which you live will not be determined by your circumstances, but by God. You must choose the "I am" identity God has prepared for you instead of the one your situation claims to represent.

You might ask, "Where in the Bible does it explicitly say that the sick should declare they are 'the healed'?" The answer is that it doesn't. Yet, if you ask, "Is there precedence in God's Word for this type of belief and confession?" To that question I can answer that there are abundant examples and a great many supporting scriptures.

Let's look at Romans 6:9-11:

> *...Christ, having been raised from the dead, dies no more. Death no longer has dominion over Him. For the death that He died, He died to sin once for all; but the life that He lives, He lives to God.*

51

Likewise you also, RECKON YOURSELVES TO BE DEAD INDEED TO SIN, but alive to God in Christ Jesus our Lord."

In this scripture, God is telling us to disavow natural reality and "reckon" ourselves dead to sin. *Reckon* in this verse means "to think, regard, consider, or believe." In spite of the fact that we have a sin nature and are prone to lust and temptation, God is saying "regard, consider," and yes, "believe" yourselves to be dead to temptation like a corpse in a casket. This is God's evaluation of how our new reality and our "I am" faith identity should respond to sin.

"Reckoning" Is Real Faith

For example, to born-again people who believe themselves to be hopelessly addicted, God is saying they are in actual fact dead to their addictions. In past chapters, I've told you that God's words often sound ridiculous. To the person who struggles—with pornography, drinking, drugs, smoking, or any addiction—and has tried unsuccessfully to break their addiction, "dead to sin" sounds ludicrous.

If you are struggling with an addiction, only one thing will work—giving legitimacy to God's Word and accepting the new reality He offers. God has "reckoned" you to be dead to sin and alive unto Christ and He is telling you to *reckon* yourself the same way.

I once pastored a church in which there was a precious brother who had a cigarette habit. I believe smokers will go to heaven, but they might get there quicker than they like. This man would come up every Sunday night to get prayer for his addiction. Every time I prayed for him I *felt* the power of God deliver him. I could see that God had set him free. Yet, after prayer he would say, "Pastor, would you pray for me at 10 A.M. tomorrow? That's coffee break time and I'll need a cigarette bad."

I knew that he would smoke again the next morning because he didn't understand that he was *already* free. I worked with him to help him believe this truth. When he came to understand and truly believe that God had already set him free in Christ, he never smoked again.

You can experience the same victory. God wants you to be free of your addiction. He has provided the means for your release, but it isn't automatic. It requires "reckoning" faith.

You might ask, "How can God tell us to reckon ourselves to be dead to sin when we have to deal with the lusts of the flesh and ungodly desires every day? The answer is that our viewpoint tends to be determined by what we experience in the *natural* realm: the things we see, feel, and think. However, God's viewpoint of us is established through the Cross. He sees us as people who are *complete* in Him.

Your course of action for deliverance is the same as mine was for healing—you must assume a new "I am" identity. You must begin to see yourself through...and identify yourself with...the finished work of the Cross.

The Cross and You

When you were born again, God identified you with Jesus' death and resurrection. The very moment you said, "Jesus, forgive me of my sins and come into my heart," something supernatural happened. Whether you felt, smelled, or tasted anything, a part of you died and was born anew.

That which died and was reborn Paul called in the book of Romans "the old man." The "old man" was a slave to sin. According to God, he now lies in a casket. The "new you" is free from slavery to sin and can choose not to be ruled by your lusts and desires. However, the devil wants you to believe that you remain under his control and that you will always be dominated by your flesh.

When you "reckon" yourself dead to sin, you are making a *real* faith statement. You're saying, I AM *"...a new creature: old things are passed away; behold, all things are become new"* (II Corinthians 5:17 KJV).

The Cross was God's elegant solution to your personal state of sin and the problems it causes. In one incredible act of love, God gave Jesus as payment in full for your sins...*potentially* undoing their effect. Yet, just as salvation was only *potentially* yours until you received it by faith, so is your deliverance from addiction, disease, and other conditions. Everything we want from God is received the same way—by faith in the fact that we are "new creations."

Think about it: Would God provide salvation from sin and not supply the empowerment to live a sin-free life? Would He command His people throughout Scripture to *"...Be holy, for I am holy"* (I Peter 1:16) and make no way for them to fulfill it? No! As a born-again person, you have access to the power to be free from *any* sickness, situation, or addiction.

The Power of Identity

Throughout the Bible, you can find people whom God instructed to assume supernatural identities contrary to their *natural* understanding. One of the best examples is Abram, whose name God changed to *Abraham*.

Genesis 17:1-5 says, *"When Abram was ninety-nine years old, the LORD appeared to Abram and said to him, '…I will make My covenant between Me and you, and will multiply you exceedingly.' …'You shall be a father of many nations. No longer shall your name be called Abram, but your name shall be Abraham….'"*

This childless, 99-year-old man with a barren wife believed God's declaration, assumed the "I am" faith identity of "father of many nations," and saw that promise fulfilled. Because he believed what God promised and acted upon it, he received his blessing, and we call him *the Father of Faith.*

When you recognize and assume by faith the "I am" identity God has declared for you, you too will receive everything God's Word says belongs to you.

God told me, an insulin-injecting diabetic, to believe and declare, "I AM the healed," and that "I AM as healed as I am saved." That was just as ludicrous as childless old Abraham calling himself "the father of many nations." Yet, it worked for him, it's working for me, and it *will* work for you.

A Faith Snare…Beware

Most of the time, when we say that we are "believ*ing*" or "trust*ing* God," it isn't *real* faith. When we add an "ing" to words like *believe* or *trust*, we somehow change their meaning. Rather than having a present-tense meaning, we have shifted the receiving into the future.

Hoping, or *future* faith, will not bring your miracle. The assertion that you are "believing" or "trusting" can be one of the biggest statements of doubt and unbelief anyone can make. Rather than a faith affirmation, it is often just the opposite, and really means, "I do not presently have what I want so I'm hoping God will take pity on me in the future."

A person who makes this kind of statement isn't "in faith"...hasn't received a rhema word from God...and hasn't come into agreement with Him. Rather, they have a desire for how things should be or have discovered a scripture that describes what they want. Then they expect God to get into agreement with *them*. Since Jesus is the *Lord* of our lives, we must come into agreement *with Him*.

When you are in close fellowship with God, you go to Him with your need, ask Him for a rhema word about your situation, agree with it, and plant your faith in what He says.

Although God's answers to prayers are often in the future, our faith *must be* that God has *already* (today, right now) answered. Look at Abram: he returned from his encounter with God and told his household to address him as Abraham. I'm sure his declaration that "I am (already) the father of multitudes" raised eyebrows. His statements probably caused people to whisper, "The old man is losing it."

Notice that Abraham wasn't a charismatic patriarch who *told God*, "I'm trusting You for a multitude of children, and my confession is 'I'm a father of multitudes.'" Rather, *God told* Abraham what to declare. Abraham then assumed the "I am" identity God gave him, and confidently asserted it.

It Works! It Works!

"I am" faith works because when Jesus died on the Cross 2,000 years ago, our sins were placed on Him and His righteousness was placed on us. Our sicknesses were put on Him and His health was placed on us. When He died, our "old man" died. When He was raised from the dead, we were raised with Him.

Now, we can walk in the same newness of life in which He walks. Ephesians 2:6 says that God *"...raised us up together, and made us sit together in the heavenly places in Christ Jesus."*

When we receive salvation, God links our identities with Christ's identity. Look at Romans 6:6: *"...Our old man was crucified with Him, that the body of sin might be done away with, that we should no longer be slaves of sin."* Also, II Corinthians 5:21 declares: *"For He made Him who knew no sin to be sin for us, that we might become the righteousness of God in Him."*

In addition, we have the promise of Romans 6:4: *"Therefore we were buried with Him through baptism into death, that just as Christ was raised from the dead by the glory of the Father, even so WE ALSO SHOULD WALK IN NEWNESS OF LIFE."* God means for us to immerse ourselves in the new identity He created for us in Christ, because victory—over sin, sickness, poverty, and much more—is found there!

Tomb Living

One day, as I sat thinking about all that God was teaching me concerning our identity in Christ, God spoke to me: "Son, do you realize that when my children continue to live in sin, they are living in a spiritual tomb? I said that they were raised with Christ so they could walk in newness of life with Christ. Yet, they want to go back to where the sin was buried.

"When people live with sickness in their lives, they too, are spiritually 'entombed.' They don't need to stay there! They need to consider divine health as something already accomplished and start accepting it, walking in it, and declaring it as done. *You don't need to live in a tomb any longer.* You were raised with Jesus into newness of life."

What exciting news! We can leave that "old man" behind and make a conscious decision to identify with the "new life" that flows through every born-again believer!

For some reading this book, I believe this is a point of decision. You know that many of the faith methods you've been taught don't work. You are looking for answers and your heart has borne witness to the truths you've read about in this book. Now God is speaking to you as He spoke to me. You must decide whether you will leave the security of the familiar (but failed beliefs) and act on these truths. Your decision will determine whether you remain in the tomb or celebrate a personal resurrection.

"I Am Who I Am"

Remember the encounter at the "burning bush" when God commissioned Moses to deliver His people from bondage? Moses asked God whom he should say had sent him to be their deliverer. In Exodus 3:14, *"…God said to Moses, 'I AM WHO I AM.' And He said, 'Thus you shall say to the children of Israel, "I AM has sent me to you."'"*

Our God is the "I Am"—present tense—God. He didn't say to them "I will be," "I could be," or "I might be" your deliverer. No! Likewise, as we walk in our new identity in Christ, our confession must be, "I am who He says I am! The 'I Am' God has declared that I AM the saved and not the condemned…I AM the healthy and not the sick…I AM the delivered and not the addicted…I AM the prosperous and not the deprived. Not I will be, but *I am!*"

I've understood "I am" faith for years concerning finances. I've walked in the identity that *"I am* the blessed." The fact that our church is debt-free and that my children, my grandchildren, and I walk in prosperity are all proof of God's financial blessing. Yet, only now have I come to understand that healing, deliverance, and *every promise* of God *also* requires "I am" faith.

Principle of *real* faith: *Faith requires us to assume the new "I am" identity which was established for us on the Cross.*

Not Tape-Recorder Faith

Some who read this book will think they now know the "formula" for *real* faith—just confess "I AM the healed, the prosperous, the delivered, or the whatever." Yet, merely speaking a truth doesn't build faith. If it were that easy, you wouldn't have to have a relationship with God—a knowledge of the Bible would be enough. Speaking faith phrases and knowing the Bible will not, by themselves, create faith. Faith arises from a personal "word" from God *specifically* for your need.

Please remember that I didn't come into my healing by merely confessing words someone told me to say or by repeating scriptures I heard on a tape. I spent hours in the presence of God, crying out for answers. God spoke to my heart, I came into agreement with Him, and faith for my miracle was born.

Perhaps God has spoken to your heart through this chapter and you have come into agreement with Him. You recognize that Jesus died, was buried, and raised to life for your salvation from sin and all of its consequences—including sickness, disease, addiction, poverty, and any destructive situation you face. That's an important first step.

Now it's time to seek God for a personal answer to your individual situation. Spend time with Him—hours or even days if necessary—seeking His rhema word for your need. Then, regardless of what He says, come into agreement with Him.

I warn you, it will require you to assume a new and probably foreign identity, but do it. Fasten your faith to His "word"...and begin to declare that God's "word" is more *real* than your situation.

When you discover *real* faith...when you grab hold of what God has already done...when you bring it by faith into your "now"...you will find your miracle waiting—a miracle acquired simply by placing your trust in the God Who calls Himself *I AM!*

CHAPTER 6

BATTLE FAITH

I must give you an important warning: once you've heard the voice of God, received His rhema word for your situation, come into agreement with it, and taken a faith stand for your need, Satan is not going to tuck his tail and run. In fact, it's just the opposite. He will challenge your faith and attempt to steal your promise. Your sickness or situation could get worse before it gets better. You will have to do battle for your blessing. That battle is commonly called a "trial of faith."

Covenant of Faith

In this book, I've talked a lot about Abraham. As the Father of Faith, he can also teach us essential things about the *trial* of our faith.

Let me remind you that in Genesis, chapter 12, God said to Abraham, *"I will make you a great nation..."* (Genesis 12:2). Years later, in Genesis 15, God and Abraham had another conversation. During this talk, God told him, *"...Do not be afraid, Abram. I am your shield, your exceedingly great reward"* (Genesis 15:1), and God restated His promises to Abraham.

Abraham asked God how those promises could possibly be fulfilled without an heir. Once again, God promised Abraham a son and the Bible says that Abraham *"...believed in the LORD, and He accounted it to him for righteousness"* (Genesis 15:6).

When God declared that He would be Abraham's shield, Abraham recognized that God was speaking *covenant* words. Abraham then asked God for a sign, a tangible expression of His promises. God told Abraham to prepare a heifer, a goat, a turtledove, and a pigeon.

Abraham understood the significance of God's request. He knew that when these animals were slain and cut in half, they were part of a ceremony that would establish his covenant relationship with God.

"Fowl Play"

In our society, we know very little about covenant *relationships* because they have been replaced by impersonal legal contracts. The only covenant we know much about is that of marriage. Although the marriage covenant has become diluted in modern society, I think most husbands still feel that their role toward their wives includes being a "shield" or protector to them—much like God promised Abraham.

Abraham prepared the animals for the ceremony as God had directed. He cut the larger animal carcasses in half and placed them opposite each other, leaving an open path down the middle. While he waited for God to ratify the covenant by walking between the slain animals, the Bible says that *"...vultures came down on the carcasses, [and] Abram drove them away"* (Genesis 15:11).

What was happening? Beyond the fact that the vultures were hungry, Abraham's covenant was in jeopardy. For the covenant to be endorsed, God had to pass between the slain animals. Had the vultures succeeded in stealing them, the covenant would not have been consummated. Abraham had to fight for his covenant just as we must fight for *our* promises.

Like Abraham, we are in a covenant relationship with God. Our covenant was created at Calvary. The sacrifice for our covenant was Jesus, the Son of God. The promises of our covenant are far better than those of Abraham's and touch upon every area of our lives.

The devil will try to steal your promises and make it impossible for God's covenant with you to be fulfilled. You must stop him! You must protect the "word" that God has spoken into your life.

God gave Abraham a "word" about his descendants, and He has given to some who are reading this book "words" about their children. You must fight every day to keep that "word" alive and fresh in your heart. Only by persevering in your faith will you see it come to pass.

Unwelcome "Word"

During Abraham's conversation with God he not only received a *good* "word," he also got a "word" that was not so welcome. God told Abraham: "*…Your descendants will be strangers in a land that is not theirs, and will serve them, and they will afflict them four hundred years*" (Genesis 15:13). In other words, the nation God promised Abraham would require centuries to establish and would first be enslaved.

When God spoke to me about my healing, He said something *I* did not want to hear, "It will take time to drive out the disease that is in your body." We are too quick to attribute these kinds of "words" to the devil. During a service, I explained to the congregation, that God had told me my healing would not be instantaneous. Following that service, I actually had people make the ridiculous statement, "You don't have to receive that. You can be healed right now."

Somehow, we've gotten the mistaken notion that God only says what we want to hear and always does things instantly. It is clear that God knew His people would be enslaved for 400 years and allowed it to happen.

It was also His will that my healing be progressive rather than instantaneous. Could He do it instantly? Of course He could, but *often* that is not His way of dealing with the issues in our lives. Despite what you may have heard, God does use "bad things" to bring good results. He allows our faith to be tested.

Testing Place

If you don't believe that God allows the testing of your faith, then whenever something goes wrong you *must* conclude that God is powerless and that Satan is in complete control of your life.

You might ask, "Why does God allow testing?" I'm not sure I have the entire answer to that question, but I believe I have a degree of understanding. Let's look at Job.

You may remember that the book of Job opens with a behind-the-scenes peek into a meeting in heaven between God and Satan. During this meeting God says to Satan, *"Have you considered My servant Job, that there is none like him on the earth, a blameless and upright man, one who fears God and shuns evil?"* (Job 1:8).

Some claim that tragedy came to Job as a result of his fears. If that had been the case, the devil would have initiated the conversation about Job and said, "Look at your servant Job. He has fear, so now I can have him." Yet, when you read Job, you'll find that the devil could only do to Job what God allowed. God was in control throughout Job's testing.

An Altar of Faith

Let's look again at Abraham. Now, it is many years after the making of his covenant with God, a time when his son Isaac was perhaps eighteen to twenty years old. God told Abraham, *"…Take now your son, your only son Isaac, whom you love, and go to the land of Moriah, and offer him there as a burnt offering…"* (Genesis 22:2).

Abraham obeyed; he didn't question, complain, or argue with God. He took Isaac to the mountain and together they prepared the altar for sacrifice. Isaac noticed there was no animal to sacrifice and when he questioned his father about it, Abraham said, *"…My son, God will provide for Himself the lamb for a burnt offering…"* (Genesis 22:8). This faith statement proved not only prophetic for Abraham, but for all mankind.

When Abraham laid his son on the altar to be sacrificed, I believe that Isaac's faith was as strong as Abraham's. Abraham raised the dagger, but before he could plunge it into the heart of *his* son, God stopped his hand.

Just as God provided a way of escape for Abraham and Isaac during their time of testing, He has promised to provide the same for you and me: *"…God is faithful, who will not allow you to be tempted beyond what you are able, but with the temptation will also make the way of escape, that you may be able to bear it"* (I Corinthians 10:13).

Visual Faith

There is something very curious about the passage of scripture that describes what happened on Mount Moriah in the moment that

Abraham almost sacrificed his son:

> *But the Angel of the LORD called to him from heaven and said, "Abraham, Abraham!" So he said, "Here I am." And He said, "Do not lay your hand on the lad, or do anything to him; for NOW I KNOW that you fear God, since you have not withheld your son, your only son, from Me."*
>
> Genesis 22:11, 12

The question is: "Didn't God 'know' *before* Abraham took the knife to slay his son that he feared and trusted God?" The Word says that God knows our hearts (I Samuel 16:7), so He surely knew what was in Abraham's heart. It also says that God knows our thoughts (Matthew 9:4). So, what was God *really* saying?

The Hebrew word translated *know* in this scripture means "to ascertain by seeing." In other words, God wasn't content to "know" Abraham's heart and thoughts, He wanted to see Abraham walk in faith. God wants to see us walk our faith out, too. God gets real pleasure watching His people living by faith in their everyday lives. *"But without faith it is impossible to please Him…"* (Hebrews 11:6).

Bicycle Faith

When I mentioned to my wife that God enjoys seeing us live by faith, she replied, "Are you saying that God lets us go through difficult times because He gets pleasure out of seeing us live through them by faith? That makes God sound uncaring."

I've thought about that and I believe that God enjoys watching us live by faith in much the same way a father enjoys teaching his children to ride a bike.

If you've had children, you know firsthand that at a certain age, usually between three and five years old, they want to learn to ride a bike. After you get the bike, you attach training wheels and they rock back and forth as they ride. Then as the child develops a sense of balance, you raise the wheels.

I'll never forget the big day when I took off the training wheels for my son. Because I knew he would probably fall, I strapped on his helmet, elbow and kneepads. Then I ran alongside the bicycle until he got his balance. Eventually, the moment came when I turned the bike loose and he rode by himself. I held my breath as he swerved and swayed down the street. When he eventually fell, I ran to see if he had hurt himself and to help him up from his *first* crash. Then I told him what a great job he'd done on his *first* ride.

Even though you know your child will probably fall the first time, and possibly several times thereafter, you teach them how to ride a bike. Why? You know two things: they need to learn this skill and the day is coming when they'll ride by with a big smile and say, "Look, Dad, no hands!"

You teach your child to ride a bicycle in spite of inevitable cuts and bruises, because you know that success is worthwhile and will bring great joy and new confidence. When they succeed, it brings you great joy, too.

So it is with your *heavenly* Father as He teaches you the vitally important skill of "riding by faith." He knows that you can never grow in faith if He puts a protective cocoon around you. So the Lord allows trials, tests, and difficult times. He wants us to be strengthened and prepared for the battle zone in which we live. We face a vicious enemy who despises and wants to destroy us.

It's War!

If you've read your Bible, you know the faith walk is not a picnic in the park. If you think it's a cakewalk, you are in denial. We face a powerful supernatural foe who detests mankind in general and Christians in particular. Satan is the worst sort of bigot; he hates you and me solely because we were created in the image of his archenemy, God. The more active you are in seeing souls saved—personally and with your prayers and finances—the more of a target you become.

Let there be no mistake, Satan will try every way he can to destroy you, your spouse, your children, and everything that belongs to you. Your only hope is *real* faith in a *real* God.

If you weren't in a war, you wouldn't need armor. Look at Ephesians 6:11-17. This passage is like a war briefing that describes your protective gear, combat weapons, and battle plan:

Put on the WHOLE ARMOR OF GOD, that you may be able to stand against the wiles of the devil. For we do not wrestle against flesh and blood, but against PRINCIPALITIES, against POWERS, against the RULERS OF THE DARKNESS of this age, against spiritual hosts of wickedness in the heavenly places. Therefore take up the whole armor of God, that you may be able to withstand in the evil day, and having done all, to stand. Stand therefore, having girded your waist with truth, having put on the breastplate of righteousness, and having shod your feet with the preparation of the gospel of peace. ABOVE ALL, TAKING THE SHIELD OF FAITH with which you will be able to quench all the fiery darts of the wicked one. And take the helmet of salvation, and the sword of the Spirit, which is the word of God.

Doesn't this scripture sound something like a father outfitting and preparing his child for their first bike ride?

Ephesians 6:18 continues the war briefing with instructions to pray *"...always with all prayer and supplication in the Spirit, being watchful to this end with all perseverance and supplication for all the saints."*

Your enemy, Satan, is very powerful, works invisibly, uses unsuspecting people, has no scruples or mercy, is totally evil, and has targeted you with missiles for destruction. Yet, *you can be supremely confident of victory!* The living God, maker of heaven and earth, has allowed a test you can handle and He holds your hand all the way through it. He has equipped and enabled you to deal with *anything* Satan shapes and hurls against you. He has promised, *"No weapon formed against you shall prosper..."* (Isaiah 54:17).

You have God's armor and you hold in your hand the mighty shield of faith that comes with a guarantee to "quench ALL the fiery darts of the wicked one." Not only can you defend yourself and withstand the enemy's attack-with real faith you can go on the offensive and take back what has been stolen. God hasn't equipped you for a stand-off...He has outfitted you to win!

Faith in your *rhema* word is your shield of defense. Proclaiming your "word" against the situation is your offensive strategy. The *"sword of the Spirit, which is the word of God,"* is your God-given *rhema* word for this trial. When you speak that "word" into your situation—the devil is eventually toast. Stick a fork in him—he's done!

Although the outcome of your fight is already determined and your success is assured, you must *engage* in the conflict to win it. Remember what God told Joshua before the battle of Jericho? *"Be strong and of good courage..."* (Joshua 1:6). The only way you can lose is to give up your faith.

Faith founded in your rhema word will bring you victory *every time!* You can trust God's battle projections because He knows the end from the beginning; He's the author and finisher of your faith. The outcome is *already* determined...you *will* win the war and enjoy success against your foe...and God will have great pleasure watching you succeed.

Precious Faith

First Peter 1:7 says, *"That the trial of your faith, being much more precious than of gold that perisheth, though it be tried with fire, might be found unto praise and honour and glory at the appearing of Jesus Christ"* (KJV).

The King James translation of this scripture can be misunderstood to say that the *trial* of your faith is *precious*. Nothing could be further from the truth. Rather, your *faith* is precious.

When you look at the Greek meanings of the words "trial" and "tried," the truth becomes clear. *Trial* refers to "trustworthiness" and the word *tried* means "to be tested or approved." Let's look at this scripture again. Now we can see that it means, *"That the* [trustworthiness] *of your faith, being much more precious than of gold that perisheth, though it be* [tested and approved] *with fire, might be found unto praise and honour and glory at the appearing of Jesus Christ"* (KJV).

When you successfully go through tests and trials, the "trustworthiness" of your faith is not only proven to God, it is proven to you. God calls your faith more precious than gold and cherishes it because it brings victory to you and "praise, honor, and glory" to His Son. Every time your faith is tested and found true, you confirm that the victory of the Cross has been successfully transferred to you.

Your faith should be very "precious" to you, too. Faith will not only bring you healing and all of God's promises but it is essential for your salvation. Guard it against the one who would steal it like your life depended on it—*"...the end of your faith* [is] *the salvation of your souls"* (I Peter 1:9).

Faith's Final Victory

Perhaps you knew a person who believed for healing, yet died. Maybe you stood in faith for someone who did not recover, or you lost a faith battle that was important to you. Because of a seeming failure of faith or the loss of a loved one, you may be tempted to give up the faith walk, grow angry with God, or abandoned the Christian life altogether.

Every trial, tribulation, misfortune, and bad situation the devil brings into your life is for one purpose—to cause you to doubt God's goodness and surrender your salvation.

Remember what Job's devil-influenced wife tried to persuade her husband to do? She exhorted him, *"…Do you still hold fast to your integrity? Curse God and die!"* (Job 2:9). That is the devil's message to you and his ultimate purpose in sending you trials. He wants you to give up on God…cast aside your faith…curse God…and die in a sinful state.

Your loved one, if they were born again when they died, won faith's final and greatest battle and they now live in total victory. The *real* faith they had in the Lord Jesus Christ as their Savior traveled with them through life and death. It whisked them into the arms of Jesus, where all pain, sickness, and suffering ended.

The greatest faith victory of all is the final one—the victory over death and hell: *"…Death is swallowed up in victory. O Death, where is your sting? O Hades, where is your victory?"* (I Corinthians 15:54, 55).

Don't let *anything* keep you from your final victory. God isn't willing that *"…any should perish but that all should come to repentance"* (II Peter 3:9). Satan's aim is the opposite. So, the final and most important faith battle for each person is not for prosperity, covenant blessings, precious promises, or even divine healing…but for their soul.

Many born-again people through the ages, and even in our time, lived and died without understanding the "faith walk." Consequently, they never experienced the full measure of victory God provided for them. Yet, if they *lost every faith* battle along the way, but kept their faith in Jesus as Savior until death, they *won the war*.

If you have disagreed with every word in this book, *you must believe this:* Every man and woman will one day be questioned by their Creator. He won't ask you if you lived in health or blessing. God will ask the final and most important question of your life: *"Did you receive Jesus as your Savior?"* If you haven't received Him...or if you have compromised your beliefs and stepped back...or even if you have renounced God-you can seek Him NOW with *real* faith and receive salvation!

CHAPTER 7

WAITING IN FAITH

In this chapter, I want to discuss what to do while you wait for your miracle. Previously, we talked about spiritual warfare. We learned how to withstand the devil's attack and take back what he has stolen. Let there be no mistake, spiritual warfare is an important part of "waiting." Yet, it isn't the only thing you need to do during the interval between getting your "word" and receiving your miracle.

Here's the scenario I'm addressing: You have established an intimate relationship with God and asked Him for a rhema word for your need. You have received that "word" and are in agreement with it. You've resolutely planted your faith in His "word," and proclaimed it.

Now you are waiting for God's "word" to be made manifest. Perhaps it will come quickly, yet often we have to wait. So, the question is: What should you to do while you wait?"

Inner Warfare

There are times when you must take the fight to the enemy. In these "seasons" you must battle him for your promise. Some would tell you that you must spend *every* waking minute in intense spiritual warfare. In reality, that would be too exhausting and could cause you to burn out. The fact is, you don't have to *constantly* engage the devil to get your victory.

Sometimes we act as though our miracle is in Satan's hands and we must wrestle it away from him through spiritual warfare. Actually, God has *already* given you your miracle. It will come into your life, not when the devil releases it, but as God's timing dictates.

For most of us, the toughest battle we face isn't with the devil, but with our mind and emotions. Because your mind and emotions aren't saved, they can become willing accomplices to the devil's aim to derail your victory.

Satan cannot actually steal your miracle. He is powerless to prevent God's "word" from coming to pass. However, *you* can rob yourself of your miracle by giving up.

You might think, "I'd never do a dumb thing like that." Yet, your mind and emotions can betray you. They can discourage you and convince you to quit rather than wait. Therefore, it is imperative that you keep your mind "renewed" to God's promise and beware of those things that would steal it away.

Robber of Miracles—Distraction

The wise man Solomon said, *"Catch us the foxes, the little foxes that spoil the vines, for our vines have tender grapes"* (Song of Solomon 2:15). Faith can be tender and vulnerable. We are all subject to "things" that would nibble away and spoil our faith. One of these "little foxes" is *distraction.*

Distraction is one of the devil's most effective strategies to steal your miracle, and perhaps the most common reason people don't receive from God. You can be distracted by—circumstances, by those around you, by your emotions, and even by human reasoning.

I'll remind you of an example from my own life. The devil and my natural mind questioned repeatedly, "How can you say, 'I *am* the healed' when the doctors say you *are* a diabetic who must inject insulin everyday?"

If you are standing in faith for your finances you might hear something like: "How can you say, 'I am *the* blessed' when every day your mail box is brimming with bills you can't pay?"

The *natural* world will entice you to doubt your rhema word and attempt to exalt itself above the Word of God. If you toy with negative thoughts, your faith will become diluted. Eventually, God's promise will take a backseat in your thinking. You must guard the promise by reacting quickly to the enemy's talk, much like a high-powered attorney would defend an innocent man from the gas chamber.

Challenge natural facts with God's truth. *Declare* that your God-given truth overpowers the natural. *Speak* God's Word and *confess* your faith. This isn't spiritual warfare with the devil. Rather, it is winning the battle within your mind. You must convince your mind "beyond a reasonable doubt."

Until the verdict is in, continue to confess your rhema word and quote scripture. You really are *the* healed, blessed, or whatever God has promised. While you wait for your miracle, you must *keep yourself* strong in faith and stubbornly refuse to allow *anything* to be lifted higher than the truth God has given you for your situation.

The Bible admonishes, *"Therefore do not cast away your confidence, which has GREAT REWARD. For you have NEED OF ENDURANCE, so that after you have done the will of God, you may receive the promise"* (Hebrews 10:35, 36). Once God has spoken something to you, it *will* happen *if* you don't "cast away" your faith.

Robber of Miracles—Time

Another hindrance to receiving is the expectation of immediate results. Sometimes God answers prayer immediately, but more often He doesn't. We need to "expect" God to answer at *any* moment, *but* not allow ourselves to become discouraged if He doesn't answer in *this* moment.

The way you prevent "time" from stealing your miracle is to make a decision to *endure until you receive.* I once heard a lady state she had waited seventeen years for a promise to be fulfilled in her life. Some might say that she sure had to wait a long time for God to move. Yet, look at the alternative. What if she hadn't endured in faith for her promise to be fulfilled? The same period of time would have elapsed, but she would have missed her miracle. Was the miracle worth the wait? She thought so. We need to be determined to endure in faith.

Waiting Can Be Resting

Consider this: When Jesus lay in the tomb, He wasn't quoting scripture or making faith confessions—He was *resting in faith*. He died confident that God would keep His Word and empower Him for the challenges that lay ahead.

Although Jesus had finished His mission on earth, He had yet to disarm Satan. In addition, Jesus was believing God for a personal miracle that was still in the future—His resurrection. Yet, for Jesus this was a time to "rest." The same is true for you and me—there's a time to rest and a time to fight. They are two distinct aspects of standing in faith.

You might ask, "How could Jesus rest knowing what lay ahead?" Have you ever played the children's game where someone stands behind you and you are supposed to fall back into their arms? This is harder than it looks, because you must know and trust the person who is catching you. You must be confident that they really intend to catch you and that they are strong enough to keep you from falling. You can only rest in God when you truly trust in Him.

Trusting and Waiting

The bottom line is—waiting requires trust. You must be totally convinced of God's good intentions toward you as stated in Jeremiah 29:11: *"For I know the thoughts that I think toward you, says the LORD, thoughts of peace and not of evil, to give you a future and a hope."*

You can't successfully "wait" for your miracle unless you have "trust" in God—a confidence in His goodness, His love and good intentions toward you. You can read about trust, speak trust, but until you have a close relationship with God, you won't *know* trust.

Trust comes out of *relationship*. The Bible says, *"...Taste and see that the LORD IS GOOD, blessed is the man who trusts in Him!"* (Psalm 34:8). You must know God to trust Him and out of trust will come your blessing.

Do you see how everything comes back to relationship with God? For God, the Cross was all about restoring the intimate relationship broken with mankind through Adam and Eve's sin. The purpose of dealing with sin was to reconcile every man and woman to an intimate relationship with God. Sadly, many people who have found salvation have never enjoyed a close relationship with the Savior.

God's purpose was to get back into relationship with mankind. So, it shouldn't seem unusual that to successfully walk in faith, God would require a close relationship with us. God wants to walk and fellowship with you daily just as He did with Adam and Eve in the garden.

Hope and the Logos Word

In Chapter 3, I've contrasted faith and hope and told you that hope would never bring your miracle. I don't want to leave you with the impression that hope is wrong, bad, or unscriptural. Actually, the word hope is found throughout the Old and New Testaments and many scriptures admonish us to have hope.

The problem is that we've confused hope with faith and thought that building hope and building faith were the same thing. "Hope" is good and necessary to faith. In fact, to successfully wait for your miracle, you *must* have hope.

Where do you get hope? You find it in God's Word. So far, I've emphasized the importance of getting God's *rhema* word for your need. I haven't yet talked about the "logos" Word of God, which is the Bible.

The logos Word is a powerful force. The Bible says, *"For the [logos] word of God is living and powerful, and sharper than any two-edged sword, piercing even to the division of soul and spirit, and of joints and marrow, and is a discerner of the thoughts and intents of the heart"* (Hebrews 4:12).

We need God's logos Word to live the Christian life and we certainly need it to walk by faith. The logos Word will build hope. I like what Psalm 119:114 says: *"You are my hiding place and my shield; I HOPE IN YOUR WORD."*

Hope and Faith

Remember with me the first part of faith's most famous scripture, Hebrews 11:1: *"Now faith is the substance of things hoped for,...."* Hope precedes faith. If you think things seem hope-*less*, then you won't go to God for the rhema word to have *real* faith for your miracle.

Here's how it works: when you read God's Word or hear a sermon based on the logos Word, hope is inspired in your heart. Godly hope is found as His Word informs you of His promises. In my case, I knew that the logos Word included divine healing, and that hope made it possible for me to pursue God for a rhema word for my healing.

In addition, God can make a logos Word become your rhema word. Perhaps you've had this happen: you were reading God's Word and suddenly you read something that seemed to leap off the page into your heart. You *knew* that God was speaking directly to you through that scripture. Indeed He was. God was making logos into rhema—giving you a personal word.

Through God's Word, you receive spiritual understanding—of Who God is…His relationship to you…what your relationship to Him should be…and what He has provided for you.

"Understanding" helps convince your mind not to give up on faith. If you don't have an understanding of what God has already done for you according to His Word, your mind can sabotage your promise.

This prayer in Psalms captures a truth for those who have a rhema word for a miracle: *"Remember the WORD to Your servant, upon which You have caused me to HOPE"* (Psalm 119:49). The Bible and your rhema word work synergistically to reinforce your hope while you wait for your miracle. Put God's logos along with His rhema words in your heart.

Peace and Waiting

Romans 8:6, says, *"For to be carnally minded is death, but to be spiritually minded is life and peace."* If you are not experiencing "peace" while you wait for your miracle, something is wrong. The problem could be your focus. When your mind is preoccupied with the "natural" perspective only, you are being "carnally minded." That can cause feelings of fear, despair, and hopelessness.

For God's peace to reign in your heart, peace must rule over your fears and emotions. Isaiah 26:3 holds the key to living in peace while you wait, *"You will keep him in perfect peace, whose mind is stayed on You…."* The word *stayed* means literally or figuratively to "lean upon or take hold of." Your mind will *naturally* lean to considering your problem, but you must redirect it to your miracle. Fear is caused when your mind "leans" in the wrong direction. Proverbs 3:5, pointedly states, "...*Lean not on your own understanding.*"

Meditate instead on God and His promise to you. Your emotions will follow your thinking. If you're fearful, your mind is centered on frightening thoughts. Control your feelings of fear by controlling your mind. When your mind is focused on the *natural*, God's supernatural solutions seem far away and impossible, and despair can result. Yet, when you keep your mind on God's good intentions toward you, His "word" to you, and the truth in the logos Word, you can know peace while you "wait" for your miracle.

When God Fights

There have been times when I couldn't fight the devil because I was too weary, weak, or sick. At those times, God fought for me and He will do the same for you. God promises that, "...*He will not let you be tempted beyond what you can bear...*" (I Corinthians 10:13 NIV).

The Old Testament tells of a time when Israel faced a great army, a seeming impossible foe. Israel was hopelessly outnumbered. God said to King Jehoshaphat, "...*Do not be afraid nor dismayed because of this great multitude, for THE BATTLE IS NOT YOURS, but God's*" (II Chronicles 20:15).

There will be times when you feel you can't fight any longer. You've done everything you know to do and your miracle is still off in the future. You might be tempted to give up. Instead of giving up...give the situation to God. There are times when you must stop "doing," and start trusting.

You might ask, "How can I know whether I should fight or rest?" When you keep a strong relationship with God, you will know because God will tell you.

There is another lesson in this Old Testament story. Do you remember what Jehoshaphat did on the day of battle? Second Chronicles 20:21, 22:

> ...*He appointed those who should sing to the LORD, and who should praise the beauty of holiness, as they went out before the army and were saying: "Praise the LORD, for His mercy endures forever." Now when they began to sing and to praise, the LORD set ambushes against the people...*"

Did you notice that God acted when they began to praise and worship? There is a lesson in that.

Praise—the Bodybuilder of Faith

Is your faith faltering? Start *exercising* to build up your faith; begin to praise God for your miracle. You cannot passively wait for your miracle and just hope it will come. Waiting in faith must be *active*.

Let's look again at Abraham to see how he spent his time waiting for his promise of an heir to be fulfilled. Romans 4:20 says, *"He did not waver at the promise of God through unbelief, but was STRENGTHENED IN FAITH, GIVING GLORY TO GOD."* Abraham didn't have "couch-potato faith." While he waited, he praised and gave glory to God. We *must* do the same.

Praise and worship are the very best things you can do while you wait. They are mighty weapons at your disposal. In fact, if you don't know what to do while waiting for your miracle—praise and worship God. You will accomplish several very important things.

Praising God for your miracle and worshiping Him as Your provider keeps God's promise fresh in your *mind*. It keeps you expecting your miracle. Praise and worship also affirm that you have come into agreement with God concerning your situation. When you praise the Lord, you are acting on *real* faith.

Do you think God would prefer that we spend our time rebuking the devil or praising Him? You can't make a mistake by praising and worshiping God.

Principle of *real* faith: *Praise and worship encourage and express real faith.*

The Power of "Impossible"

Recall with me the Day of Pentecost recounted in the second chapter of the book of Acts. When the Holy Spirit was poured out on those gathered in the upper room, it created such a commotion that a large crowd gathered to find out what was taking place.

Peter, speaking for the 120, reminded those who had assembled that the Jews had recently crucified Jesus. Then he told them of Jesus' resurrection:

> *Whom God raised up, having loosed the pains of death, because it was NOT POSSIBLE that He should be held by it. For David says concerning Him: "...For You will not leave my soul in Hades, nor will You allow Your Holy One to see corruption."*
>
> Acts 2:24-27

Take special notice of the phrase *"...It was not possible that He should be held by it* [death]." Why do you suppose it was not possible for death to hold Jesus? The reason is simple: God had declared through David that it was *im*-possible. God *said* that He would *not* leave His Son in Hades nor allow His body to decay in death. Once God had spoken, it became *impossible* that Jesus could remain dead...and it is just as impossible for you not to receive the manifestation of God's "word" to you IF you endure.

The Jesus-Kind-of-Faith

A Biblical illustration of enduring faith is found in Hebrews 2:8. It says of Jesus, *"'You have put all things in subjection under his feet'....But now WE DO NOT YET SEE ALL THINGS PUT UNDER HIM."*

When you and I look around at our world almost 2,000 years after this was written, we see this promise *still* unfulfilled. The fact is, very few things are submitted to Jesus' control. Entire governments and people are not subject to Him, and the devil and his demons are running rampant across the earth.

Do you suppose that Jesus is leaning over and whispering in the Father's ear, "It isn't working"? Jesus is like us in that He, too, is standing in faith with a *rhema* word about His future.

Hebrews 10:12, 13 gives us a snapshot of Jesus today and shows us just what He is doing while He waits for His rhema word to be fulfilled: *"But this man [Jesus], after he had offered one sacrifice for sins for ever, sat down on the right hand of God; from henceforth EXPECTING till his enemies be made his footstool"* (KJV). Jesus is waiting expectantly for the fulfillment of God's Word.

We are called *Christians* because we are "people like Christ," so we must do the same. Hang onto God's "word" and wait expectantly for its fulfillment. The Bible describes our situation perfectly in Romans 8:25 where it says, *"But if we hope for what we do not see, we eagerly wait for it with perseverance."* In other words, you've got to hang in there because God works by His schedule, not ours.

Galatians 4:4, says that Jesus' first coming to earth happened in the "fullness of time"—that's God way. God considers all the factors and moves when the time is exactly right. Because only God can know all the elements of the situation, you and I can *never know* when He will send our miracle. So, we've got to hang onto our faith and wait expectantly.

Principle of *real* faith: *Real faith must be enduring faith that waits expectantly, as long as it takes, to receive the promise.*

Facsimile of Faith

I must make this point one final time: the attempt to reduce real faith to a formula is a recipe for calamity. A good example can be found in the book of Acts. Recounted there is the attempt by the seven sons of Sceva to cast out a demon. When they tried to make a formula of something someone else had done successfully, it failed miserably.

They said to the demon-possessed man, *"…We exorcise you by the Jesus whom Paul preaches"* (Acts 19:13). The demon replied, *"'…Jesus I know, and Paul I know; but who are you?' Then the man in whom the evil spirit was leaped on them, overpowered them, and prevailed against them, so that they fled out of that house naked and wounded"* (Acts 19:15, 16).

Formulas have no power. In fact, they are dangerous. Words, even God's Word, spoken by rote without the backing of real faith, are empty of supernatural power. It is faith, not mere words, that focuses God's miracle-working power on your need.

Formula faith is ineffectual. It can leave you defeated and spiritually stripped. On the other hand, when your actions are prompted by your relationship with God and based on His "word," you will always be successful.

The End of Waiting

I want to remind you that whether you have to "wait" ten minutes or ten years for your victory, you *will* get your miracle if you refuse to give up!

The Psalmist declared: *"...For You have magnified Your word above all Your name"* (Psalms 138:2). There is no name higher or power greater than God's. Yet, God has backed His "word" for your miracle above His name. By doing so, He has staked His very integrity upon the assurance that your rhema word from Him is true and reliable.

Just as God vowed and kept His word to raise Christ from the dead, He has pledged by His name to keep the "word" given to you. And, He will use the very same miracle-working power that raised Jesus from the dead to do it.

Resurrection power is aimed at your need. Your *real* faith has released it into your situation. Just as that power could not fail to raise Jesus from the dead, it will not fail to give you the miracle God has promised. Don't give up on your rhema word!

CHAPTER 8

THE REAL TRUTH ABOUT HEALING POWER

While I was learning how to have real faith to receive my healing, the Lord also taught me the scriptural basis for healing and living in divine health. *It isn't what you might think!* This teaching goes beyond our traditional healing scriptures and penetrates to the very core of our New Covenant rights.

During that time of instruction, God taught me the greatest healing scripture in the Bible and it doesn't mention the word "healing." Yet, our "entitlement" to healing and divine health rests squarely upon its fundamental truths.

This chapter is not about how to have *real* faith. Rather it explains *why* we can have faith for healing, divine health, and other things. Whether you are standing against killer diseases as I was, or pressing through for any other seeming impossible situations, you will need more than a list of scriptures. You need a firm footing or understanding of God's provision for your need.

This chapter explains the doctrine of healing taught by Paul to the early church as related in the Book of Ephesians. As you may know, it is generally believed that someone other than Paul founded the church in Ephesus. When he heard of this church, Paul was eager for them to have a clear understanding of their fundamental "rights" as believers. Hence he wrote the passage we will study.

The Greatest Healing Scripture

The most powerful healing scripture in the Bible is Ephesians 1:15-23. When you get hold of this truth, healing and divine health become easier for your mind to understand.

Let's take a look at this scripture verse by verse. It begins: *"…After I heard of your faith [I]…do not cease…making mention of you in my prayers:* (Ephesians 1:15, 16).

The first thing to notice is that Paul didn't start praying for the Ephesian Christians *until* he heard of their faith. Keep in mind that this reference has nothing to do with praying for the unsaved. Paul is talking about prayer for Christians who have faith in God—as opposed to "believers" who have no faith to receive from God.

I've laid hands on some people for healing and it was like praying for a post—nothing spiritual happened. I've laid hands on others and felt God's anointing flow into them. The only difference between them is that some had faith and others didn't. Only faith can draw on God's power for healing.

A Touch of Faith

Luke 8:43-48 tells of the time a large crowd surrounded Jesus as He headed to Jairus' house to pray for the man's daughter. In the press of the crowd, a woman with an "issue of blood" touched the hem of Jesus' garment. Her touch stopped Jesus in His tracks and He said, "Who touched me?" Jesus' disciples replied, "Everyone is touching you!" Jesus explained that this was a *special* touch saying, "I felt virtue flow out of me."

The faith of the woman with the issue of blood was a demanding force that drew on Jesus' power for healing and miracles. Jesus confirmed that her faith had released the miracle when He said to the woman, "Your faith has made you whole."

Hundreds, perhaps thousands, must have touched Jesus' skin and clothing that day. Some probably brushed against His shoulders; other may have patted His back or grasped His hand. I'm sure everyone who touched Jesus was, like you and me, a person with some kind of need. Many of them must have hoped that merely touching Jesus would bring a miracle.

Yet only the woman, who did not touch His skin, but only the edge of His garment, received a miracle. Why? It's obvious: she touched Jesus with faith for her need. The others failed to receive because they only touched Him with hope.

Today, as Jesus stands at the right hand of the Father, He still has the power to heal. He is waiting for *your* touch of faith. The power for your healing will be released by your faith.

Crucial Revelation

As the scripture in Ephesians continues, we find Paul praying specific things for the Ephesians. He prayed that they would receive a very important revelation. This is the same revelation we need, to receive our healing: *"That the God…may give to you the spirit of WISDOM AND REVELATION IN THE KNOWLEDGE OF HIM"* (Ephesians 1:17).

The English word *revelation* is used for three Greek words with three different meanings. In this passage, the word for revelation is *epiphaneia*, which refers to Jesus' first coming to earth, His Resurrection from the dead, and its implication for mankind. Our healing and other covenant rights are linked to the success of Jesus' first mission to earth.

Another Greek word, *parousia*, is also translated "revelation" and it refers to Christ Second Coming. A third word translated in Scripture as "revelation" is *apokalupsis*. This is where we get our word apocalypse and it refers to the changes that will affect mankind and the earth when Christ comes again.

So, in this verse, Paul is saying, "I'm praying that the eyes of your understanding will be opened and that you will realize the *implications* of the first coming of Jesus."

"Might" That Is Rightful

To fully understand the *implications* of what Jesus has already accomplished, you must know that during the millennia between Adam's sin and Christ's arrival on earth, this planet and its people were under the absolute control and authority of Satan.

When Adam and Eve were tempted by Satan and sinned in the Garden of Eden, their sin had devastating and long-lasting consequences: it allowed Satan to usurp Adam's God-given power, authority, and dominion over the earth. Instead of man being the master of earth as God intended, Satan, the fallen archangel who aspires to replace God, became its cruel commander.

Ephesians 1:21, explains the spiritual power structure that developed on earth under the rule of Satan: "...*power and might and dominion,....*" The word *power* used in this passage refers to the devil's power and the Greek lexicon defines it as, "might that is right or authority that is lawful." This word points out that Satan had *legal* power and authority over our planet.

One of the things Jesus came to do was to strip Satan of his authority. The Bible says in Colossians 2:15 that "*Having disarmed principalities and powers, [Jesus] made a public spectacle of them, triumphing over them in it.*" When Jesus "disarmed" the devil, He revoked his authority over sin, sickness, disease, and death.

This is a place to get excited! Do you see that the devil lost his *legal right* to put sickness on you? Don't misunderstand: the sickness Satan gives you isn't merely a "symptom." It's genuine. Satan didn't lose the actual *power* to make you sick. He lost the right to make you sick.

You, on the other hand, gained the right to live in divine health. The scripture we're studying is the declaration of your victory over cancer, heart conditions, diabetes, and any other disease or condition the devil has given you. What Satan has done to you is not only wrong—it is illegal!

Called to Conquer

As we continue our study in Ephesians chapter one, Paul tells us that we need to understand the incredible thing God has accomplished through Christ:

> *The eyes of your understanding being enlightened; that you may know what is THE HOPE OF HIS CALLING, what are the riches of the glory of His inheritance in the saints.*

> Ephesians 1:18

You are "called" to do something awesome; however, this calling isn't to a kind of ministry. Rather, this is your calling to exercise power and authority.

Ephesians 1:18 begins to explain your calling by defining it as, *"…the riches of the glory of His inheritance in the saints."* This is exciting! You are called to take possession of your inheritance and I can't wait to tell you about it.

The word *glory* in this verse means exactly that, "glory." I point that out because another Greek word often translated *glory* in the Bible means "dignity or honor."

Speaking of dignity, there is none attached to sickness and disease. If you have spent any time as a hospital patient, you know what I mean. When you're in the hospital, you might as well leave dignity at home.

As I was being wheeled on a steel gurney down a hospital hall for open-heart surgery barely covered by a hospital gown, I was thinking, "This is horrible. I'm the only one here with no clothes on; everyone is fully clothed but me."

Just then I heard a little voice say, "Pastor, I want you to know we're praying for you." I was very glad people were praying, but completely mortified that anyone from my church was present to see their pastor during this embarrassing moment. Later, I told my wife, "I don't know who that person was and you must never tell me." There is no honor or dignity whatsoever in disease.

Faith's Inheritance

Getting back to your glorious "inheritance": I hope you don't think that your inheritance only involves going to heaven when you die. As crucially important as that is, there is *much more* to your inheritance. In fact, a good deal of your inheritance is in effect *right now*.

You were not saved to struggle through life, nobly bearing up under sickness and other attacks of the enemy against you and your family. No! Your inheritance endows you with certain *inalienable rights*.

Endowment of Power

Now read Ephesians 1:19-20 very carefully as Paul defines our inheritance:

> *...And what is the exceeding greatness of His POWER toward us who believe, according to the working of His mighty POWER which He worked in Christ when He raised Him from the dead....*

Remember, I told you that your inheritance is one of power. The first word used for power in this passage is the Greek word *dunamis*, which you may know means "miracle-working power." It is the same word used in Acts 1:8 where it states, *"...You shall receive power when the Holy Spirit has come upon you...."*

Notice in Ephesians 1:19 the phrase: *"...what is the exceeding greatness of His power...."* The words exceeding and greatness are used to describe His miracle-working power. The Greek word for "exceeding" in this scripture is *hyperballo*, which means "to go beyond the mark, to far surpass or excel." The Greek word for "greatness" is *megethos*, which in English becomes "mega or huge."

When we plug our new understanding into the verse it reads: *"...And what is the* [far-surpassing] [hugeness] *of His* [miracle-working power] *toward us who believe...."* God has given us power that goes beyond miracle-working power. It is a power so huge it surpasses any other and is greater by far than the devil's power.

Because it is an inheritance, this power is the legal right of *every Christian.* It has been given to you to use against Satan and every demon that would oppose your "right" to healing and health. This power and authority doesn't *originate* in you, but in God. Yet, as a born-again believer, it can flow through you to your needs by means of *real* faith.

Think about it: you have authority over *every* power of hell. Yet, like so many spiritual things, it isn't automatic and you can't use it anyway you like. This power is activated by the faith your *rhema* word generates. *Real* faith is the means by which you direct this commanding force to *enforce* your God-given rights.

In the Cross-Hairs of Power

"And what is the exceeding greatness of his POWER TO US-WARD who believe, according to the working of his mighty POWER" (Ephesians 1:19: KJV).

Notice where God's power is aimed: it is pointed *"...to us-ward who believe..."* (KJV). This incredible power has you in its sights. The word *believe* in this verse means "to respect as to a person." This tells us that God's power is available to those who respect the *person* of Jesus.

You might ask, "What is the 'person of Jesus'"? It is the sum total of Who Jesus is, and what He accomplished on earth and in heaven. The more we understand and believe what Jesus accomplished for us through His death and resurrection, the better we can target this formidable power at our illness and other needs.

The remainder of the verse describes the nature of the power to which we have access: *"...According to the working of His mighty power"* (Ephesians 1:19).

Now we know that this power isn't just any kind of manifested power: it is "mighty." The Greek word translated "mighty" is *ischus*. A derivative of this word, *ischou*, means "strong in body, whole, and healthy." An aspect of this mighty power is focused on your health. The Greek word used for the second word translated "power" is *kratos*, which means "manifested or operative power."

So, when we gather up our expanded understanding of this verse and apply it, this passage of scripture tells us: "We Christians have inherited a miracle-working, health-giving, operative power."

Resurrection Power

I have a great illustration for this. Think of a massive thunderstorm filled with rumbling thunder with lightening bolts spraying in every direction. If we could take all of that storm's tremendous energy and concentrate it on a single spot on the ground, imagine what it would do.

A power greater than the strongest thunderstorm or, for that matter, any other power in the universe IS focused on believers. This power can be manifested in healing and strength for our physical bodies.

This tremendous power is further described as the same power *"…which He worked in Christ when He raised Him from the dead…"* (Ephesians 1:20). This power is life-giving and so great that it was able to return life to Jesus' dead body.

When Jesus hung on the Cross, all of our sicknesses were placed on Him and He carried them to death for us. Yet, when the miracle-working power of God touched Jesus' body and raised it from the dead, He conquered not only death but every sickness and disease He carried.

When Jesus arose from the dead He didn't say, "I'm alive but I don't feel too well." No! Jesus shouted triumphantly, *"I am He who lives, and was dead, and behold, I am alive forevermore. Amen. And I have the keys of Hades and of Death"* (Revelation 1:18).

Power Points

Let's recap what we've learned about faith and healing from Ephesians 1:15-23:

1. You need faith to receive healing.

2. Your faith draws on Jesus' power to heal.

3. You must have a revelation of what Jesus accomplished by His death and resurrection.

4. Your disease is "unlawful"; the devil's authority to make you sick was taken away by Jesus.

5. You have an inheritance in Jesus: the "right" to exercise power over sickness and the devil.

6. You are "called" to exercise this power.

7. You have God's awesome power aimed at you.

8. You have a mighty, miracle-working power at your disposal.

9. Your health and healing needs are a rightful target of this power.

10. The power at your disposal is the same great power that raised Jesus from the dead.

Power Picture

Imagine this: You are standing under a cloudless sky. God's awesome power is shining down on you. It is brighter than the sun. You take your need to God; He gives you a *rhema* word for your situation. Your agreement with Him triggers a shaft of power that beams down…strikes your shield of faith…and is reflected at your need. Since nothing can withstand that blaze of power, your need vanishes in a puff of smoke.

This is a word picture designed to help you see the powerful position you have as a Christian, but the truth it illustrates is *not* a parable. For at this very moment, God's mighty power is in truth focused on *you*. Use it!

AFTERWORD:

A STORY OF GOD'S FAITHFULNESS

God is faithful even when we're stinkers. No matter how long you've been a Christian, you can mess things up and make mistakes. You will never get *everything* exactly "right" until you get to heaven.

If we are honest, we recognize that we have shortcomings. We might think that because we're flawed, God will be faithful to others (people better than we are) but not to us. We might even believe that we must earn God's faithfulness and makeup for our shortcoming by "doing" things.

Yet, in Psalm 89:1, the psalmist rejoices over the connection between God's mercy and His faithfulness: *"I will sing of the MERCIES of the LORD forever; with my mouth will I make known Your FAITHFULNESS to all generations."* God's faithfulness rises out of His mercy. We must learn that our actions—good or bad—will not cause God to change His ways.

Second Timothy 2:13 says, *"If we are faithless, He remains faithful; He cannot deny Himself."* This scripture means that faithfulness is the very nature of God. Dogs bark because they're dogs; eagles soar because they're eagles, and God is faithful because that's the way He is. God is changeless, despite our failures.

I am living proof that God's faithfulness is linked to His mercy. During the years after my heart surgery, I went through some of the darkest spiritual times of my life. I came to the place where after decades of ministry, I thought about giving up. My health, my credibility, and my faith were suddenly in question, and the answers were nowhere to be found.

A Hole in the Hedge

Before 1994, my life flourished. I felt like Job before his trials—there was a hedge of protection and blessing around me. Everything I did was successful. Then in 1994 my father died and two years later, I was diagnosed with diabetes. Diabetes wrecks your life—it lays waste to your health and emotions.

Not long after that diagnosis, I was skiing and felt chest pains. I went to a cardiologist and had a treadmill test that showed something was wrong. When I scheduled my angiogram, I told my doctor I had to get this fixed quickly because I was going to Israel the following week.

After the procedure, the doctor informed me that my arteries were nearly 100% clogged. He said it was a miracle that I hadn't had a heart attack already and that I needed bypass surgery immediately!

I reminded him of my travel plans: "I'm leaving for Israel on Monday; when I return I'll call you." He looked at me sternly and said, "Pastor, I don't think you understand the seriousness of your condition. If you go to Israel in your present state, one of two things *will* happen: you'll either end up in a foreign hospital or return home in a body bag." Needless to say, he had gotten my attention. Instead of going to Israel on Monday, I had open-heart surgery.

Following the surgery, I was truly thankful to be alive. I remember telling God, "As long as there is breath in my lungs, I will praise you!" Soon, however, I began to experience deep depression. It was unlike anything I had ever known.

The Mark of a Leader

My depression had two causes: First, I was very troubled about the "bad" example I was setting for my congregation. I've always believed that a leader leads by example. As far as I'm concerned, actions are more important than any sermon you can ever preach. You either "live the life" or you don't; you are either a *real* man of God or you aren't. I have always endeavored to be such a man.

Yet, concerning healing and health, I felt I was a bad example, a person who didn't know how to follow God in the area of healing. My inability to have faith for healing made me feel unqualified to lead. I wanted to give up my pulpit. It was an incredibly difficult time.

The second cause for my depression was the mistrust and even anger I had developed toward God. Those feelings consumed every moment of every day and fueled my depression. I was at war with God and accused Him of unfaithfulness to me. I questioned how He could have allowed this illness to happen to me.

Some people believe and teach that if you have enough faith, bad things can't happen. That is not true. I admonish you to *never* put that kind of guilt trip on a person. It is very easy to make those accusations when you aren't the one suffering. It's an allegation that doesn't help, but only hinders another's faith.

My God, like Job's, allowed sickness and disease to come upon me. He had a purpose and reason for my sickness and, as He did with Job, God had a date for my deliverance. Yet, in the midst of the trial, I could see no possible benefit from my illness.

It was a time of torment for me. You *know* things are bad when the pastor doesn't want to go to church. I went, but when I got there I didn't feel like praising and worshiping God. I believed that I didn't have much of a relationship with God or a reason to praise Him and I certainly didn't want to get up and preach.

Then…Things Got Worse

One Sunday when I came home from church, my wife, Linda, asked me how the second service had gone. I told her, "If you're going to minister nowadays, you'd better be prepared to be a Jeremiah." Jeremiah, as you know, was the weeping prophet who preached forty years without a single convert.

It was a ridiculous statement, especially considering that eight people were born again in that service. Yet, when you're depressed everything seems wrong. My attitude towards God had begun to color my outlook. As a result, my staff and my wife lived with a difficult person for a *long* time.

That Sunday, Linda looked at me across the table and said, "I don't want to be Jeremiah's wife. Maybe you need to resign. I'd rather be a checker at a grocery store than continue to live like this." When we returned to church that evening for service, she told me, "I'm not going to the service. I've had it!" I went to my office to prepare for the service and then began to wonder if Linda had gone home.

I looked for her car and discovered that it was still in the parking lot. So I searched and finally found her in an empty office, weeping. "John," she cried, "something has to change! We can't go on like this." All I could say was, "I don't know how to change it." Have you ever been there? If you have then you know there are times when you can't just reach down and pull yourself up by your own bootstraps.

You should understand that I am completely devoted to my wife. Her happiness is very important to me. I would do *anything* for her. Yet, this time all I could do was admit that I was a pastor, a husband, and a believer who couldn't even help himself. My depression deepened.

On the following Tuesday, one of my pastors, Diane, came to my office and asked to talk with me. She said, "I was praying this morning and God gave me a scripture for you. Pastor you may fire me after you read it, but I have to be faithful to God," and she handed me the scripture.

It was the Amplified Version of Jeremiah 15:19: *"Therefore thus says the Lord [to Jeremiah]: If you return [and give up this mistaken tone of distrust and despair], then I will give you again a settled place of quiet and safety, and you will be My minister; and if you separate the precious from the vile [cleansing your own heart from unworthy and unwarranted suspicions concerning God's FAITHFULNESS], you shall be My mouthpiece...."*

I asked Pastor Diane if she had been talking to my wife. She said, "Pastor, I don't know what you are talking about." When she left, I called Linda and accused her of talking to Diane. She said, "John, I swear before God that I haven't breathed a word of this to anyone."

I could no longer deny this was a word from God for me, and fell to the floor of my office. I wept and repented for accusing God of being unfaithful. I vowed to Him that regardless of what happened in the future, I would *never again* charge Him with unfaithfulness.

The Battle Begins

I wish I could tell you that my health got better after this event, but just the opposite happened—it became worse. My diabetes progressed to the point that I was forced to take insulin injections. Then, the following spring, I tested positive for another deadly disease, lupus. Now, I became desperate with God. I realized that unless I received a healing miracle, I would not have much longer to live.

> Over a period of three months, God spoke three very clear words to me. They were my *rhema* words for healing that I've told you about: God told me that He would satisfy me with long life...it was OK to say that I was the healed, and that I was as healed as I was saved. I had a very hard time believing these "words" from God because I had, not one, but three incurable diseases—heart disease, diabetes, and lupus.

Then God gave me the scripture in Isaiah 53:1, *"Who has believed our report?...."* He whispered in my mind, "You've believed the report concerning your salvation, but you haven't believed the report concerning your healing."

I was reminded by the Holy Spirit that I am saved whether I act like it, talk like it, or think like it. He showed me that the same principle applied to my body. God said that my body *was* healed. He taught me that regardless of how I felt or what the outcome was of any test—I will always *be* the healed!

The light bulb went on and I began to praise God for my healing. Two weeks later, I had my doctor run the tests for lupus again. This time the results were different—my body showed no trace of the disease. God had healed me!

The Lord began to talk to me about my diabetes. He said it wouldn't go away instantly, but would leave one step at a time. That was hard to hear because I was very weary of diabetes. I was taking 52 units of insulin per day. Over the next few months, my need for insulin began to decrease until I was down to 21 units per day. There it remained for many months.

The Faith of a Child

Then one Sunday morning my three-year-old grandson, Jordan, ran into my office. This loveable and shy child said to me with great boldness, "Papa, I need to pray for you."

I had no idea what he would pray. When I said, "OK," he came over, put his hand on my knee and prayed, "Jesus, help Papa not to need shots." He added a hurried "Amen," and dashed out the door.

In the hall, Jordan encountered my wife and told her, "Nana, Papa not need shots—I prayed." The next day, I experienced hypoglycemic events caused by low blood sugar. That meant that I was taking too much insulin. By that evening, I had to cut my insulin intake in half. The next day, I had to eat all day because my blood sugar continued going lower and lower.

The following evening, when it was time for my injection, I checked my blood sugar level. At 61, it was so low that an injection of insulin could have killed me. I told my wife, "I can't take my insulin tonight;" and we shared a meaningful look. *I haven't taken a shot since.*

A month later, I returned to my endocrinologist for a scheduled check-up. When I showed her the log of my blood sugar readings, she was excited. "Those are the best numbers you've ever had" she exclaimed. When she asked for my insulin log, I told her I didn't have one because I hadn't taken any injections during the month.

She looked shocked; then immediately ordered a hemoglobin A1C test. You can fake your insulin log, but blood tests reveal the truth. When I was taking three shots a day, my best hemoglobin test was 6.7. A non-diabetic will have a count of between four and six.

When the test results from the hemoglobin A1C came back she said, "This is a miracle!" "As a matter of fact," I replied, "You're exactly right." Then I told her about a three-year-old boy who had responded to God and prayed for me. Since his simple prayer, I have been able to throw away my insulin and needles because Jesus has, in fact, "healed Jordan's papa."

Faithful…Faithful…Faithful

Through the LORD's mercies we are not consumed, because His compassions fail not. They are new every morning; great is Your faithfulness.

Lamentations 3:22-23

God is so *very* faithful. No matter what we do, He remains faithful to us and to His Word. His faithfulness will not change regardless of what you say or do. Think about it—hasn't God brought you through past difficulties?

Don't become nearsighted and see only the problems of today. Instead, look to the good plan He has for your life. Seek God in your time of need. Hold on to the things He has promised…*never let them go.* Your healing, the salvation of your children, your prosperity—whatever God promised—will come to pass because He is forever faithful!

I believe with all my heart that God allowed me to go through my illness and write this book about *real* faith for you and the others it will touch. Whatever crisis you're facing—health, financial, or any other kind—God is telling you that He will be faithful to you, too! He will walk with you through your situation, however devastating, and bring you to the other side in victory.

If you have read to this point, but haven't begun seeking God for your need, isn't it time to lay down this book, and cry out to God? If you will pursue God for a *real* faith miracle, the end of my story can be the beginning of yours!